Contents

MATERIALS

Fabrics and interfacings

The main fabric you choose for your stumpwork embroidery can be any fabric you desire. In seventeenth century England, silk, satin and fine linen canvas were frequently used.

If you select a fabric with a pile, such as velvet, you may find that the thread will be partially covered by the pile. To overcome this, use thicker threads, more strands of a thread or denser stitches. If you choose a printed fabric, ensure the pattern has been printed on the grain. It is disappointing to complete an embroidery and then find that a skewed pattern or skewed grain detract from the finished piece.

Because the fabric needs to support detached objects, slips and often dense embroidery, it is important to use a backing fabric. Quilter's muslin is commonly used but any firm, natural fabric can be substituted. Fabrics such as calico, poplin and homespun are excellent alternatives. A thin layer of padding, such as Pellon, can be placed between the main fabric and the backing fabric. This can add dimension to the surface embroidery and also diminishes the effect that tails of wire may have on the front.

Interfacings can be utilized to give body to fabrics used for slips and detached elements. Fusible interfacings will also help prevent these pieces from fraying. Heavy upholstery interfacings are excellent for slips where a hard edge is required. Felt is commonly used for padding and slips. It is easily moulded and does not fray.

Threads

Any threads from the glorious range available today can be used for stumpwork. Natural threads, made from cotton or silk, are generally easier to use than synthetic threads. These often seem to have a mind of their own and are more susceptible to becoming fluffy and worn. Metallic threads often feature in stumpwork and as these threads wear easily it is best to work with only short lengths.

Wire

The fine wire used by cake decorators is the most versatile for stumpwork and is the wire most commonly used in this book. It is available in different gauges or sizes, and can be covered or uncovered.

30 gauge covered wire is available in several colours, but most commonly white and green. This paper wrapped wire can be easily coloured with pencils, paints or felt-tipped pens. It is easier to stitch over than uncovered wire as the surface is not so slippery.

28 gauge uncovered wire is a silver coloured wire that is actually thicker in diameter than 30 gauge. Without the paper covering it gives a finer effect. Uncovered 30 gauge wire can be too flimsy to hold its shape when stitched.

34 gauge beading wire is very fine but can be used for delicate objects such as insect wings.

Beads

We are so spoiled with the vast range of beads available to us and any can be incorporated into your stumpwork embroidery. Larger beads can be wrapped or covered with needlelace to become any three-dimensional object you choose, or simply used as they are. Smaller beads, such as the extensive ranges from Mill Hill and Delica, can be used individually, clustered or strung together.

Found objects

Historically shells, feathers, coral, carved wood, pearls, semi-precious stones, seeds, leather, beetle wings and all manner of found objects were used to embellish stumpwork embroideries. Slivers of mica were frequently used to depict glass windows.

Today we can add to this list with all sorts of buttons and delightful little charms, shisha mirrors, sequins, jewellery findings or whatever takes your fancy.

TOOLS

Needles

A variety of types and sizes of needles are utilized in stumpwork to cater for the wide range of stitches and threads used. Each design within this book is accompanied by a list of the required needles and information about when and where to use them. Generally speaking, the thread should be able to pass easily through the eye of the needle.

Beading needles

As their name suggests, these long slender needles are used for beading. They bend easily so always stitch with a 'stabbing' rather than a 'scooping' motion.

Crewel needles

Crewel needles, with their large slender eye, thin shaft and sharp tip, are the most commonly used needles for embroidery.

Chenille needles

Chenille needles are similar in appearance to crewel needles but have a thicker shaft and are generally shorter. Large chenille needles are also suitable for sinking wires.

Darners

Both long and yarn darners are heavy duty needles that are suitable for sinking wires and for stitching with thick or chunky threads.

Straw (milliner's) needles

Straw needles have a long, fine shaft and a small eye that is no wider than the shaft. They are suitable for

beading and working knot stitches such as bullion knots and drizzle stitch.

Tapestry needles

These needles are similar to chenille needles but have a blunt tip. Use them when it is important not to split the thread of previous stitches or for stitches that incorporate whipping or weaving.

Hoops

Hoops or frames are essential for stumpwork. The fabric needs to be held 'drum' tight if the finished project is going to be free from puckers and distortion. Hoops that can be tightened with a screwdriver will hold the fabric more firmly than spring hoops. Binding the inner ring of a hoop also aids in achieving a firm tension on the fabric. It is also kinder on your fabric than an unbound hoop. Wooden hoops tend to grip the fabric much better than metal or plastic ones.

Because so much of stumpwork embroidery is raised or padded, it is important to use a hoop large enough to hold the entire design. Once the main fabric has been mounted in the hoop it should remain there until the embroidery is complete. As hoops can permanently mark some fabrics if they are held for extended periods, a hoop or frame larger than the finished design and border will minimise the impact of such marks on your project.

If your design requires a hoop larger than approximately 25cm (10") in diameter consider using a square or rectangular frame for mounting your fabric.

Scissors

It is worth investing in good quality scissors as they make a huge difference to the ease and quality of your work. You will need a small pair with fine, sharp blades and tip for snipping threads and yarn. A larger, heavier pair is necessary for cutting fabric.

A third pair can be used for cutting wire. Never use your embroidery or fabric scissors for cutting wire as the blades will quickly become dull.

Needlelace pad

A needlelace pad, also known as a buttonhole pad, provides a support for working such stitches as detached blanket stitch and corded detached blanket stitch when they do not have a background fabric.

To make a pad, sandwich a layer of thin wadding (eg Pellon) between two pieces of medium weight nonwoven interfacing. Sandwich this between two pieces of a firmly woven smooth fabric such as poplin. Stitch around all sides to hold the layers together. Your needlelace pad can be circular, rectangular or square.

Tape a tracing of your chosen shape onto the pad and couch your foundation threads or wire to the pad through the tracing. Alternatively, hold the tracing in place with plastic wrap.

Other tools

Tweezers and pliers

Pliers are invaluable for bending and shaping wire. The small needle-nosed pliers that jewellers use are the easiest to handle for intricate work. Tweezers are also a useful item to have in your stumpwork embroidery kit. Use them for bending wires and shaping detached objects.

Brushes and combs

Ghiordes knots are often featured in stumpwork designs. To create a soft fluffy pile, the cut loops must be brushed or combed. Different embroiderers have various favourite methods that they employ. Some prefer to use a small suede brush and others prefer a very fine toothed comb or an eyebrow comb. Both methods are effective.

Thimbles

A thimble worn on the middle finger of your stitching hand can be useful for pushing the needle into the fabric before pulling it through on the other side with your thumb and index finger. A thimble should fit your finger firmly enough so that it is not easily dislodged but does not pinch your skin.

If you find you are constantly pricking yourself but find a thimble uncomfortable to wear, a quilter's thimble can be a good compromise. Made of leather with a small metal insert in the tip, they provide protection and the suppleness of the leather allows for more flexibility.

Lights

Good lighting is essential if you are to place your stitches accurately and not strain your eyes. Ensure you have a good, strong light source directed at your embroidery. Remember also that the type of light you view your threads in will affect the way they look. Unless you have exceptionally good lighting, choose thread colours in daylight. It is so disappointing to spend an evening selecting colours and stitching, only to wake up the next morning and discover that, in the light of day, they really do not go together.

Magnifiers

Magnifiers are available in a range of styles. They can clip onto your own glasses, hang from a cord around your neck or be freestanding. Some have their own light source. While they certainly make your stitches easier to see, they can make it difficult to accurately judge the length of stitches. If you use a magnifier, first establish the size and spacing of your stitches without it and then use the magnifier while maintaining the same stitch size and spacing. Occasionally view your work without the magnifier so you can see the overall effect of your stitching.

TRANSFERRING DESIGNS

Transferring designs to main fabric

There are a variety of methods and tools available to help you transfer your chosen design from paper to fabric. The method you choose will depend on personal preference, the size and intricacy of the design, your choice of fabric and stitches, and the use of the finished embroidery.

To eliminate the likelihood of the design becoming distorted as the fabric is tightened mount it in the hoop before transferring the design. Place the mounted fabric over a smooth hard surface, such as a book or tin lid, which sits inside the hoop.

Direct tracing

With this method the more transparent the fabric the easier it is to see the design. Placing a light source behind the fabric will make it appear more transparent. Use a light box or tape the design to a sun-filled window. For this method, the design is transferred before the fabric is mounted in the hoop.

Draw or trace your design onto tracing paper with black ink or a black felt-tipped pen. Tape the tracing to a flat surface (this could be your window or light box). Position the fabric over the tracing and tape in place. Trace over the design lines with a lead pencil, fabric marking pen, or chalk-based marker.

Indirect tracing

Trace the design onto tracing paper with a pencil or black pen. Turn the tracing over to the wrong side and retrace over the design lines with a fine lead pencil. Position the tracing, wrong side down, onto the right side of the fabric and tape in place. With a smooth, hard surface behind the fabric and using a pencil or empty biro, firmly trace over the design lines once more. The lead pencil lines on the wrong side of the tracing will be transferred to the fabric.

Tacking

Tacking is very time consuming but no permanent marks are left on the fabric. Trace the design onto tracing or tissue paper. Position the tracing on the right side of the fabric and pin or tape in place.

Using a thread that contrasts with the fabric colour, tack along the design lines with small even running stitches. Score the tacked lines with the tip of the needle and tear the paper away. With tissue paper, you can wipe over the design lines with a damp sponge and then tear the paper away.

Dressmaker's carbon

This is suitable for fabrics with a smooth surface and comes in several colours, so choose a colour that contrasts with your fabric. The marks are permanent.

Support the fabric, right side up, on a smooth hard surface. Place the carbon onto the fabric, waxed side down. Position the drawing of the design over the carbon and tape in place. Trace over the design lines with a sharp pencil, ballpoint pen or tracing wheel.

Transferring shapes for cutting out

Place fusible webbing, paper side up, over the template. Trace the out-line using a pencil. Fuse the tracing to the wrong side of the fabric and cut out along the traced lines. Remove the backing paper before applying the shape to the main fabric. Alternatively, trace the shapes onto tracing paper and cut out. Pin or tape the tracing to the fabric and cut around it. ✼

Safe Keeping,
Inspirations issue 34

- DRIZZLE STITCH -

 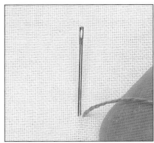 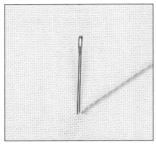 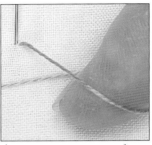

1. Secure the thread on the back of the fabric and bring it to the front.

2. Unthread the needle. Insert the needle halfway into the fabric very close to where the fabric emerged.

3. With your finger facing you, place the thread over your finger.

4. Begin to rotate your finger away from you. Keep the thread taut and looped around your finger.

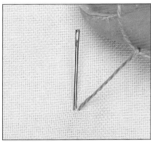 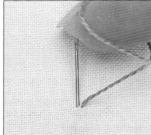 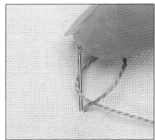 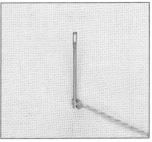

5. Continue to rotate your finger until the thread is wrapped around it.

6. Keeping tension on the thread, place the tip of your finger on the end of the needle.

7. Slip the loop off your finger and onto the needle.

8. Pull the thread tight, slipping the loop down the needle onto the fabric.

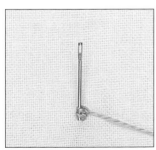 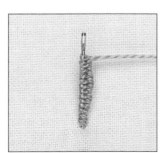  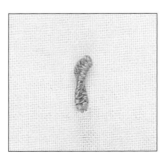

9. Again, loop the thread around your finger following steps 3 - 6. Slip the loop onto the needle and pull the thread firmly until the loop lies against the first loop.

10. Continue working the required number of cast-ons in the same manner.

11. Rethread the needle. Placing your thumb over the cast-ons, begin to pull the needle through (thumb not shown).

12. Pull the thread through and end off on the back of the fabric.

- RAISED CHAIN STITCH -

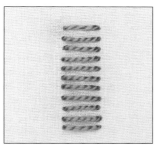

1. Work evenly spaced, parallel straight stitches to form the framework. Place the stitches approximately 1.5mm (¹/₁₆") apart.

2. Secure a new thread on the back of the fabric and bring it to the front at A, just above the middle of the first straight stitch.

3. Slide the needle from bottom to top beneath the first straight stitch, angling the needle to the left. Do not go through the fabric.

4. Pull the thread through.

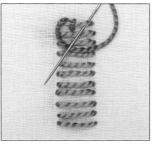

5. Loop the thread to the right. Slide the needle from top to bottom, beneath the first straight stitch. Ensure the loop is under the tip of the needle.

6. Pull the thread through.

7. Slide the needle from bottom to top beneath the second straight stitch, angling the needle to the left.

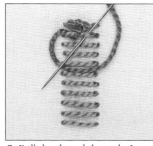

8. Pull the thread through. Loop it to the right. Slide the needle from top to bottom, beneath the second straight stitch. Ensure the loop is under the tip of the needle.

9. Pull the thread through.

10. Continue working in the same manner to the end of the straight stitches.

11. To finish, take the needle to the back of the fabric, just over the last straight stitch.

12. Pull the thread through and end off on the back of the fabric.

- RAISED STEM STITCH -

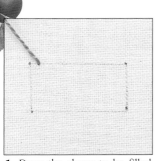

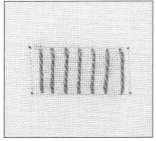

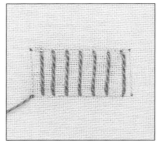

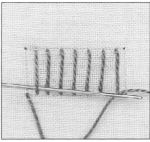

1. Draw the shape to be filled on the front of the fabric. Secure the thread on the back of the fabric and bring it to the front on the outline.

2. Work evenly spaced parallel straight stitches across the shape at right angles to the outline. End off the thread on the back of the fabric.

3. Secure a new thread on the back and bring it to the front on the lower left hand side of the shape.

4. Keeping the thread below the needle, slide the needle from right to left under the first straight stitch. Do not go through the fabric.

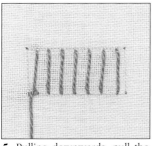

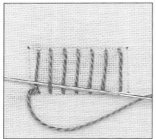

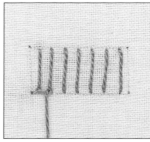

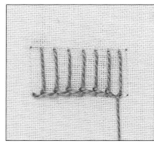

5. Pulling downwards, pull the thread through until it wraps firmly around the straight stitch.

6. Keeping the thread below the needle, slide the needle from right to left under the second straight stitch. Do not go through the fabric.

7. Pull the thread through as before.

8. Continue to the end of the straight stitches.

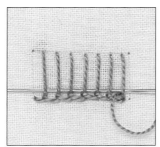

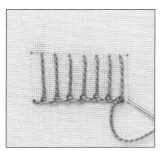

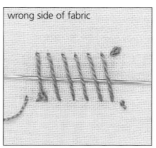

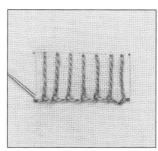

9. Slide the needle behind the straight stitches and pack down the stem stitches.

10. Remove the needle and then take it to the back of the fabric at the end of the shape.

11. Pull the thread through. On the wrong side, slide the needle under the straight stitches. Do not go through the fabric.

12. Bring the needle to the front on the left hand side just above the previous row.

- RAISED STEM STITCH CONTINUED -

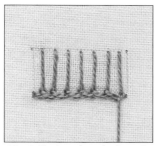 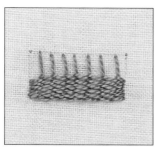  

13. Pull the thread through. Work stem stitches across the row in the same manner as before.

14. Pack down the stitches and slide the needle behind the straight stitches on the back as before. Continue working rows in the same manner.

15. After the last stitch, take the needle to the back of the fabric on the upper right hand side.

16. Pull the thread through and end off on the back of the fabric.

- CIRCULAR RHODES STITCH -

 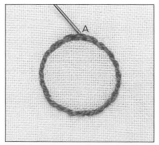 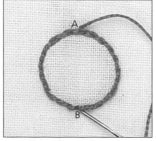 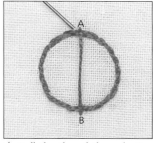

1. Draw a circle on the front of the fabric. Outline it with tiny split stitches.

2. Bring the needle to the front of the fabric at A, just outside the stitched outline.

3. Pull the thread through. Take the needle to the back at B, directly opposite A and just outside the stitched outline.

4. Pull the thread through. Re-emerge just to the left of A.

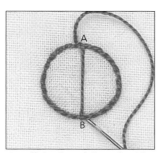 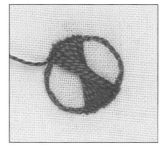 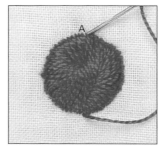 

5. Pull the thread through. Take the needle to the back just to the right of B.

6. Pull the thread through. Continue working stitches in an anti-clockwise direction, keeping them close together. Ensure stitches always start and finish on opposite sides.

7. Continue until the outline is completely covered. To finish, take the needle to the back of the fabric just to the right of A.

8. Pull the thread through and end off on the back of the fabric.

- BULLION KNOT -

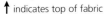 ↑ indicates top of fabric

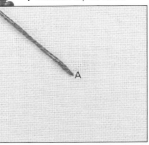

1. Secure the thread on the back of the fabric. Bring it to the front at A.

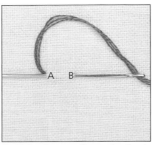

2. Take the needle to the back at B. Re-emerge at A, taking care not to split the thread.

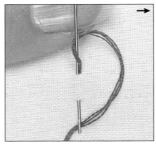

3. Rotate the fabric. Raise the tip of the needle away from the fabric. Wrap the thread clockwise around the needle.

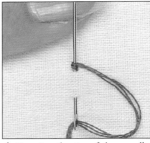

4. Keeping the tip of the needle raised, pull the wrap firmly down onto the fabric.

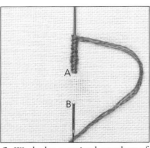

5. Work the required number of wraps around the needle. The number of wraps must cover the distance from A - B plus an extra 1 - 2 wraps. Pack them down evenly as you wrap.

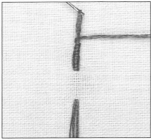

6. Keeping tension on the wraps with your thumb, begin to ease the needle through the fabric and wraps (thumb not shown).

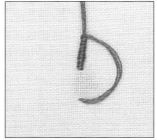

7. Continuing to keep tension on the wraps with your thumb, pull the thread through (thumb not shown).

8. Pull the thread all the way through, tugging it away from you to form a small pleat in the fabric. This helps to ensure a tight even knot.

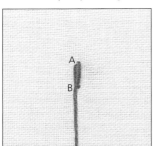

9. Release the thread. Smooth out the fabric and the knot will lie back towards B.

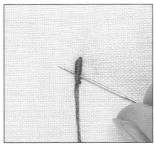

10. To ensure all the wraps are even, gently stroke and manipulate them with the needle while maintaining tension on the thread.

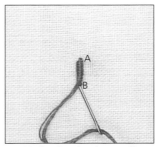

11. To finish, take the needle to the back at B.

12. Pull the thread through and end off on the back of the fabric.

- BULLION LOOP -

↑ indicates top of fabric

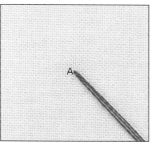

1. Secure the thread on the back of the fabric. Bring it to the front at A.

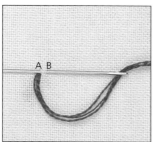

2. Take the needle to the back at B. Re-emerge at A, taking care not to split the thread.

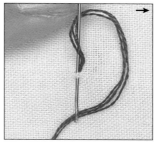

3. Rotate the fabric. Raise the tip of the needle away from the fabric. Wrap the thread clockwise around the needle.

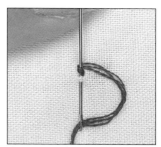

4. Keeping the tip of the needle raised, pull the wrap firmly down onto the fabric.

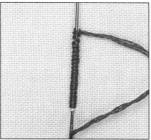

5. Work the required number of wraps around the needle. Pack them down evenly as you wrap.

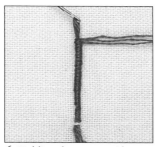

6. Holding the wraps with your thumb, begin to ease the needle through the fabric and wraps (thumb not shown).

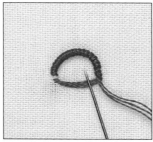

7. Pull the thread all the way through. Separate the wraps from the adjacent thread with the tip of the needle.

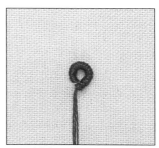

8. Hold the wraps in place with your thumb (thumb not shown). Pull the thread towards you to tighten the wraps and curl them into a tight loop.

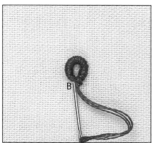

9. To finish, take the needle to the back at B.

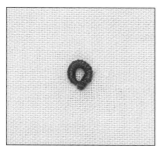

10. Pull the thread through and end off on the back of the fabric.

Hints - Bullions

1. Bullion knots and loops are very difficult to work in a hoop. In stumpwork, they are better used on a slip. This can be freely held in the hand and then applied to the background fabric.

2. Whether you are left or right handed, always wrap the thread in a clockwise direction. Thread wrapped anti-clockwise puts in extra twist and makes the bullion tighter.

- FRENCH KNOT -

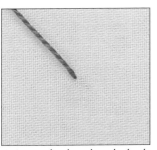

1. Secure the thread on the back of the fabric and bring it to the front at the position for the knot.

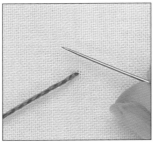

2. Hold the thread firmly approximately 3cm (1 ¹⁄₈") away from the fabric.

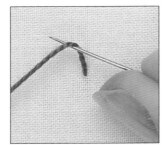

3. Take the thread over the needle, ensuring the needle points away from the fabric.

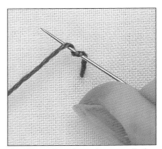

4. Wrap the thread around the needle. Keeping the thread taut, turn the tip of the needle towards the fabric.

5. Take the tip of the needle to the back of the fabric approximately 1 - 2 fabric threads away from where it emerged.

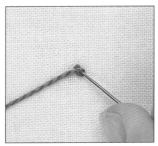

6. Slide the knot down the needle onto the fabric. Pull the thread until the knot is firmly around the needle.

7. Push the needle through the fabric. Hold the knot in place with your thumb and pull the thread through (thumb not shown).

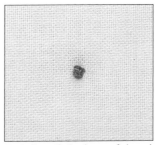

8. Pull until the loop of thread completely disappears. End off on the back of the fabric.

- GHIORDES KNOT -

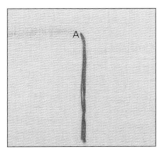

1. First row. Take the needle to the back at A. Pull the thread through, leaving a tail on the front of the fabric.

2. Re-emerge at B, just to the left of A. Take the needle to the back at C, just to the right of A.

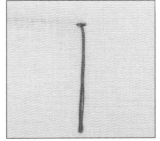

3. Hold the tail taut and pull the thread through to form a straight stitch.

4. Re-emerge at A, behind the straight stitch.

- GHIORDES KNOT CONTINUED -

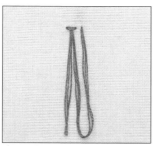

5. Pull the thread through. With the thread below the needle, take the needle to the back at D.

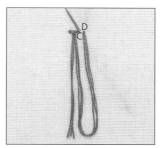

6. Pull the thread through, leaving a loop the same length as the tail.

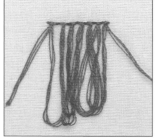

7. Hold the loop in place with your thumb and bring the needle to the front at C (thumb not shown).

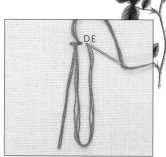

8. Pull the thread through. Take the needle to the back at E.

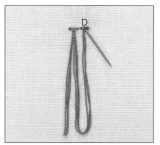

9. Pull the thread through to form a straight stitch. Bring the needle to the front at D, behind the straight stitch.

10. Pull the thread through. With the thread below the needle, take it to the back at F, leaving a loop on the front.

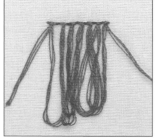

11. Continue to the end of the row in the same manner, finishing with the thread on the front. Ensure the last stitch is not a loop.

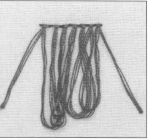

12. Trim the thread, leaving a tail the same length as the loops.

13. Second row. Take the needle to the back of the fabric directly above A. Pull the thread through, leaving a tail on the front of the fabric.

14. Work the second row in the same manner as the first row.

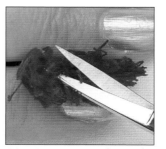

15. Continue working the required number of rows in the same manner. Stand the loops up and trim them evenly.

16. Alternate between combing and trimming until the stitches are the desired height and appearance.

- PADDED SATIN STITCH -

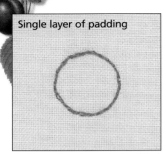

Single layer of padding

1. Draw the shape to be filled on the front of the fabric. Secure the thread on the back. Outline the shape with split back stitch.

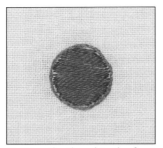

2. Bring the thread to the front just inside the outline. Work satin stitches across the shape, starting and ending each stitch just inside the outline.

3. Alternatively, work rows of chain stitch, starting and ending each row just inside the outline.

4. Secure a new thread on the back of the fabric. Bring it to the front at A, just outside the outline.

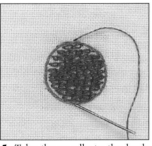

5. Take the needle to the back of the fabric on the opposite side of the shape and just outside the outline.

6. Pull the thread through and re-emerge on the opposite side, very close to A.

7. Pull the thread through. Continue working stitches in the same manner until the shape is completely covered.

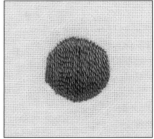

8. To finish, take the needle to the back of the fabric after the last stitch. Pull the thread through and end off on the back of the fabric.

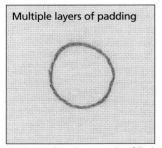

Multiple layers of padding

1. Draw the shape to be filled on the front of the fabric. Secure the thread on the back. Outline the shape with split back stitch.

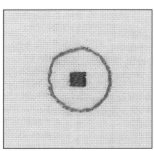

2. Work a layer of satin stitches in the middle of the shape.

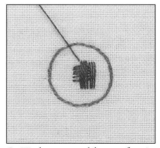

3. Work a second layer of satin stitches, slightly larger than the first layer and in the opposite direction. Keep the stitches within the outline.

4. Work a final layer of satin stitch in the opposite direction to the previous layer, covering the outline.

- TRAILING -

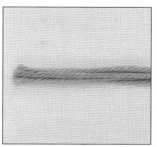

1. Position the laid threads for the padding on the front of the fabric.

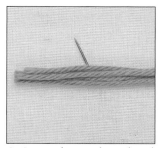

2. Secure the couching thread on the back of the fabric. Bring it to the front near one end of the laid threads, angling the needle from under the threads.

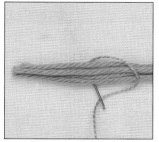

3. Pull the thread through. Take the needle to the back of the fabric on the opposite side, again angling the needle under the threads.

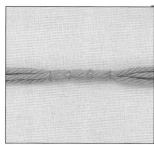

4. Pull the thread through. Continue couching in the same manner, placing stitches at approximately 5 - 10mm (3/16 - 3/8") intervals.

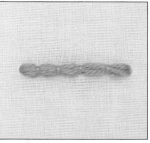

5. Take the ends of the laid threads to the back of the fabric and secure.

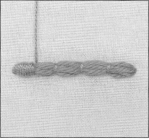

6. Secure a new thread on the back. Work overcast stitches, angling the needle in the same manner as the couching so only a small piece of fabric is picked up with each stitch.

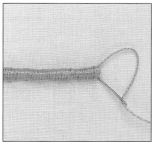

7. Continue to the end of the laid threads. To finish, take the needle to the back of the fabric behind the end of the laid threads.

8. Pull the thread through and end off on the back of the fabric.

Hints

1. Soft tapestry cotton is an excellent padding thread for trailing. Pass the required number of lengths through beeswax until they hold together or squeak. Take care not to over wax as the threads do not need to stick together. Remove the excess wax by running your fingers down the threads.

2. When couching groups of laid threads, pull the stitches firmly but not so tight that they form deep indents in the laid threads.

3. Use raised chain stitch as a filling stitch by extending the length of the straight stitches and working rows of raised chain stitch, side by side, over them.

4. Work raised stem stitch over felt padding or bundles of laid threads to further enhance the three-dimensional effect.

5. When stitching ghiordes knots, always make the loops longer than you require. This way you don't have to be so fussy about the length of each loop. It is also easier to keep the loops away from where you are stitching as they will lie down.

- SLIP STITCH -

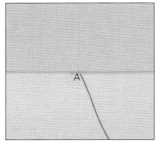

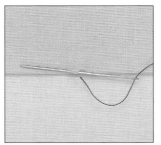

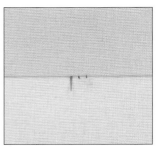

1. With right sides uppermost, position the piece to be attached onto the main fabric. Ensure the seam allowance of the piece is turned under.

2. Secure the thread on the back of the fabric. Bring it to the front at A, through the main fabric only but as close as possible to the piece.

3. Take the needle behind the folded edge of the piece. Re-emerge a short distance away.

4. Pull the thread through. Take the needle to the back and then re-emerge a short distance away through the main fabric only.

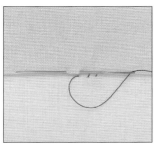

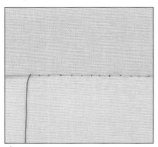

5. Pull the thread through. Again, take the needle behind the folded edge of the piece and re-emerge a short distance away.

6. Pull the thread through. Continue working stitches in the same manner.

7. To finish, end off the thread on the back of the main fabric behind the attached piece.

Winged Desire, *Inspirations* issue 37

- STAB STITCH -

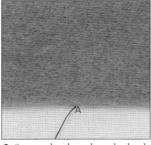

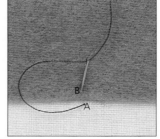

1. With right sides uppermost, position the piece to be attached onto the main fabric.

2. Secure the thread on the back of the fabric. Bring it to the front at A, through the main fabric only but as close as possible to the piece.

3. Keeping the needle at right angles to the fabric, take it to the back at B, inside the edge of the piece.

4. Pull the thread through.

- STAB STITCH CONTINUED -

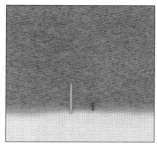

5. Again, keeping the needle at right angles to the fabric, re-emerge through the main fabric only but as close as possible to the piece.

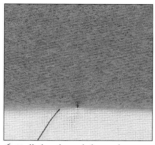

6. Pull the thread through.

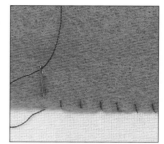

7. Continue working stitches in the same manner.

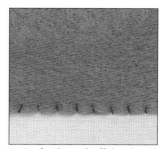

8. To finish, end off the thread on the back of the main fabric behind the attached piece.

- PADDING WITH FELT AND FIBRE-FILL -

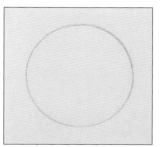

1. Trace the padding shape onto the paper side of fusible webbing. This shape will be slightly larger than the shape on the main fabric.

2. Fuse the tracing to the felt and then cut out the shape. Remove the backing paper.

3. Centre the shape, fusible webbing side down, over the marked outline on the main fabric.

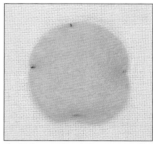

4. Using stab stitch, secure the felt to the marked outline at its extremities. The felt will not lie completely flat.

5. Continue working stab stitches around the shape, leaving a small opening.

6. Push fibre-fill through the opening, pushing it into the edges.

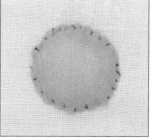

7. Close the opening with stab stitches and end off the thread on the back of the main fabric behind the shape.

8. Cover the felt with embroidery or a slip.

- LAYERING FELT -

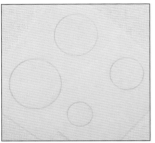

1. Trace the padding shapes onto the paper side of fusible webbing.

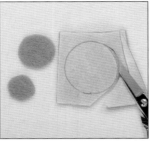

2. Fuse the tracing to the felt and then cut out the shapes. Remove the backing paper.

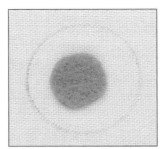

3. Centre the smallest shape, fusible webbing side down, within the marked outline on the main fabric.

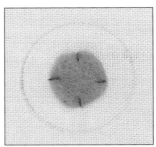

4. Using stab stitch, secure the felt to the fabric at its extremities.

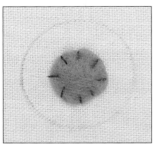

5. If required, work further stab stitches between those already worked.

6. Centre the next smallest shape over the first.

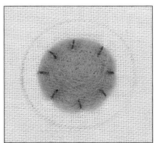

7. Attach in the same manner as before.

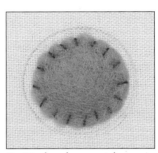

8. Attach subsequent layers in the same manner.

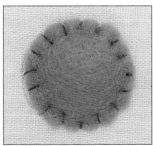

9. For the last layer, work stab stitches approximately 2mm (¹/₁₆") apart.

10. Cover the felt with embroidery or a slip.

Hints - Padding

1. Animal wool makes an excellent soft filling. Avoid using cotton wool as this can go hard and lumpy.

2. As an alternative to fibre-fill, tapestry wool, knitting wool and soft cotton can be used as a filling for trapunto. Thread the yarn into a tapestry needle. On the back of the fabric, take the yarn between the two layers of fabric. Cut the yarn after each stitch so the space between the layers fills with numerous short lengths of yarn. When the shape is filled, trim the tails of yarn on the back close to the fabric. Push the ends into the space with the tip of the tapestry needle.

- PADDING WITH LAID THREADS -

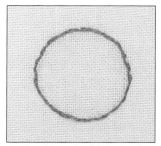

1. On the main fabric, outline the shape to be padded with a stitch such as split back stitch.

2. Lay the thread along the inner edge of the outline. Couch down, keeping the couching stitches within the shape, and spiralling the laid thread towards the centre.

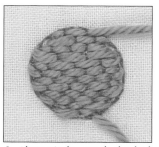

3. Alternatively, couch the laid thread back and forth across the shape.

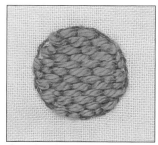

4. Take the ends of the laid thread to the back of the fabric inside the outline. Secure them on the back of the fabric behind the shape.

- TRAPUNTO -

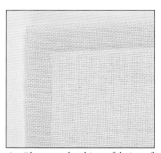

1. Place a backing fabric of quilter's muslin behind the main fabric.

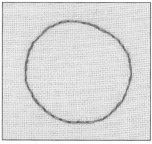

2. On the right side of the fabric, outline the shape with back stitch.

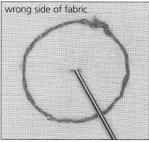

3. Turn the fabric to the wrong side. Using a tapestry needle, carefully push apart the threads of the muslin to form an opening.

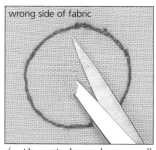

4. Alternatively, make a small cut in the backing fabric only with a pair of small sharp scissors.

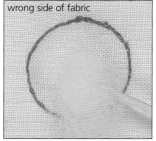

5. Push fibre-fill through the hole between the two layers of fabric.

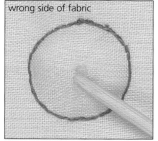

6. Use a skewer or similar to push the fibre-fill into the edges and corners.

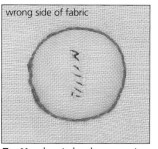

7. Hand stitch the opening closed.

8. On the right side of the fabric, fill the shape with your chosen embroidery, stitching through the top layer of fabric only.

- CREATING A SLIP -

Slips are pieces of embroidery that are worked separately to the main design and then appliquéd to it. They are often padded and are usually worked on evenweave canvas or a fabric such as calico or homespun. Slips can be knitted, crocheted, gathered or pleated and can be left unattached along one or more sides.

If your chosen fabric frays easily, leave a wider seam allowance or seal the edge with fray stopper.

Use acid free cardboard or heavy weight interfacing, such as upholsterers use, for padding hard-edged slips. Both soft and hard-edged padding can be used together. Insert the soft padding between the slip and the hard-edged padding but do not push it into the edges.

1. Transfer the design for the slip to the fabric and mount it in a hoop. Outline the shape with a stitch such as split back stitch.

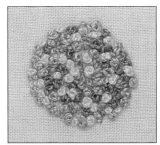

2. Fill the shape with your chosen embroidery stitches.

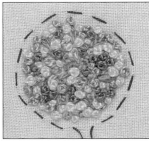

3. Leaving a tail of thread on the front, work small running stitches around the entire shape approximately 3mm (1/8") away from the outline. Do not end off the thread.

4. Cut out the shape approximately 3mm (1/8") away from the running stitches.

5. Pull up the running stitches to turn the seam allowance to the wrong side and tie off the thread.

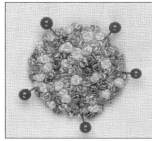

6. Position the slip on the main fabric and pin in place.

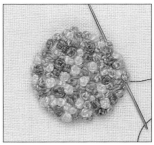

7. Following the instructions on page 18, slip stitch the slip in place.

8. To finish, end off the thread on the back of the main fabric behind the slip.

Hints - Padding

1. Use a skewer, knitting needle or large tapestry needle to push filling into the edges and corners of padded shapes.

2. When using laid threads to pad a shape, the threads can be couched down individually, in pairs or in bundles.

- P A D D I N G   A   S O F T   S L I P -

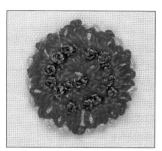

1. Attach the slip to the main fabric, leaving a small opening. Push fibre-fill through the opening, pushing it into the edges and corners.

2. Slip stitch the opening closed.

1. Add layers of felt padding to the main fabric. Position the slip over the padding and pin in place.

2. Slip stitch the slip to the main fabric.

- P A D D I N G   A   H A R D - E D G E D   S L I P -

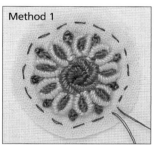

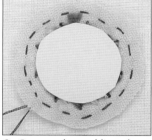

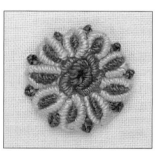

1. Work the slip following steps 1 - 4 on page 22.

2. Cut out the padding shape and place it onto the wrong side of the slip.

3. Pull up the running stitches and tie off the thread firmly.

4. Attach the slip to the main fabric with slip stitch.

1. Work the slip following steps 1 - 2 on page 22. Cut it out, leaving a 6mm (¼") seam allowance. Clip the seam allowance as shown.

2. Cut out the padding shape and place it onto the wrong side of the slip.

3. Stretch the slip over the padding and glue the seam allowance to it.

4. Attach the slip to the main fabric with slip stitch.

- SHAPING WIRE -

A foundation of fine wire will add strength to design elements that are elevated from the main fabric. Wire is utilised in many of the detached leaves, petals, wings and even ears that feature in the designs later in this book.

These photographs show the most common ways that wire is used to support fabric shapes. Of course, almost any shape can be formed. To create sharp points, squeeze the wire together with a pair of flat-ended tweezers or small pliers.

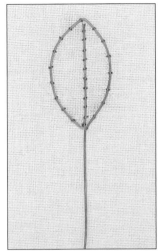

1. Couch the wire along the centre before bending it to fit the outline.

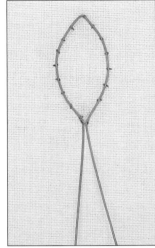

2. The wires should touch at the base but not cross over. Work couching or overcasting stitches across both wires to keep them together.

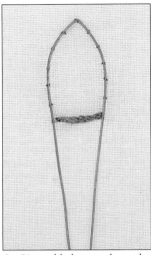

3. Give added strength to the unwired section with two rows of split back stitch.

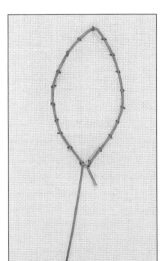

4. Trim the short tail of wire away before inserting the shape into the background fabric.

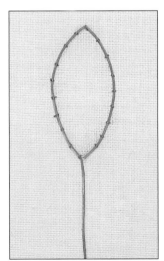

5. Ensure the start of the wire does not cross the adjacent section of wire.

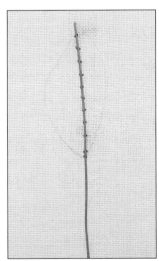

6. Attach a centre wire before embroidering the rest of the shape.

- C O V E R I N G   W I R E -

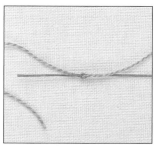 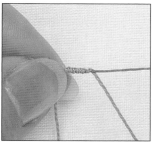 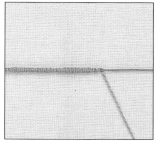 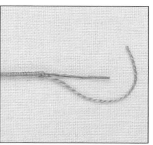

1. Knot the thread approximately 2.5cm (1") from the end of the wire, leaving a 5cm (2") tail dangling.

2. Holding the thread and wire near the knot, begin to wrap the thread around the wire. Keep the wraps close together.

3. Continue until the required distance is covered.

4. Knot the thread, leaving a 5cm (2") tail dangling. Trim excess wire 2.5cm (1") beyond the end of the wraps.

- C O U C H I N G   W I R E -

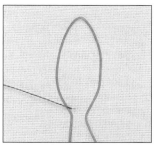 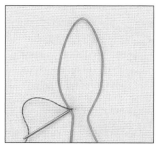 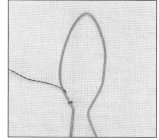

1. Secure the thread on the back of the fabric. Bring it to the front as close as possible to the wire inside the shape.

2. Keeping the needle at right angles to the fabric, take the needle to the back of the fabric on the opposite side of the wire.

3. Pull the thread through. Re-emerge just inside the shape approximately 5mm (3/16") further along the wire.

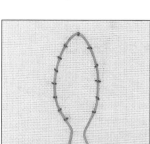 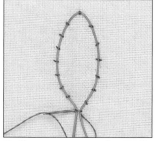 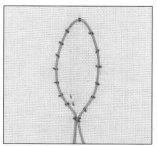

4. Take the needle to the back of the fabric on the opposite side of the wire. Continue working stitches in the same manner around the shape.

5. If two segments of wire lie close together, take 1 - 2 stitches over both wires at the same time.

6. Take the needle to the back of the fabric and end off the thread inside the shape.

Hints

1. Keep the tails of wire at least 2.5cm (1") long so that the detached shapes can be more easily manipulated and attached to the background fabric securely.

2. Temporarily stitch or tape the tails of wire down while you embroider the detached shape. This helps to prevent them catching your threads while stitching.

- C O I L I N G   W I R E -

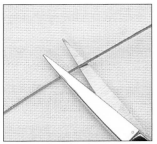 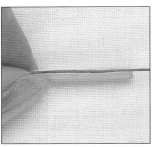 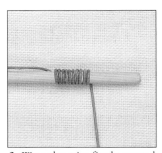 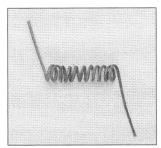

1. Cut a length of wire at least three times longer than the required finished length plus 5cm (2").

2. Leaving a tail of 2.5cm (1"), hold the tail along the shaft of a long cylindrical object such as a large needle, skewer or pencil.

3. Wrap the wire firmly around your chosen object until 2.5cm (1") from the end of the wire. Keep the wraps close together.

4. Slide the coil off the cylinder. It is now ready to attach to the background fabric.

- O V E R C A S T   S T I T C H -

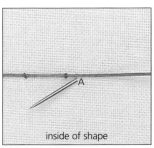 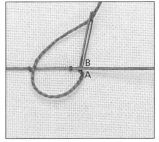 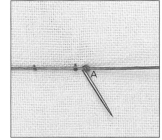

1. Secure the thread on the back of the fabric. Keeping the needle at right angles to the fabric, bring it to the front as close as possible to the wire inside the shape (A).

2. Pull the thread through. Again, keeping the needle at right angles to the fabric, take the needle to the back of the fabric on the opposite side of the wire (B).

3. Pull the thread through. Again, keeping the needle at right angles to the fabric, re-emerge very close to A.

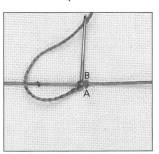 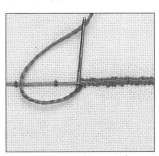 

4. Pull the thread through. Take the needle to the back of the fabric on the opposite side of the wire very close to B.

5. Continue working stitches in the same manner, incorporating the couching stitches into the line of overcast stitches.

6. When the wire is completely covered, take the needle to the back of the fabric and end off the thread inside the shape.

Hints

1. Large chenille needles and yarn darners are the most suitable needles to use when inserting wires.

2. When cutting out wired shapes, angle your scissors so the lower blade is just under the stitches and the upper blade is angled away from them.

- BLANKET STITCH -

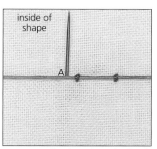

1. Secure the thread on the back of the fabric. Keeping the needle at right angles to the fabric, bring it to the front at A, just inside the wire.

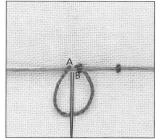

2. Pull the thread through. Take the needle to the back of the fabric close to where it emerged.

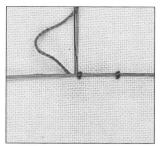

3. Pull the thread, leaving a small loop on the front. Bring the needle to the front at B, inside the loop.

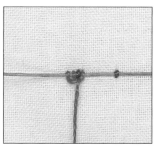

4. Pull the thread through until the loop lies snugly against the emerging thread.

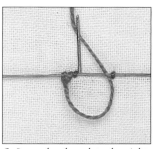

5. Loop the thread to the right. Keeping the needle at right angles to the fabric, take it to the back of the fabric just inside the shape.

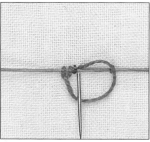

6. Pull the thread part way through and re-emerge on the other side of the wire within the looped thread.

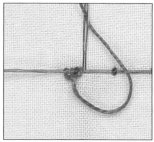

7. Pull the thread through until the loop lies snugly against the emerging thread.

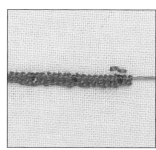

8. Loop the thread to the right again. Take the needle to the back of the fabric inside the shape in the same manner as before.

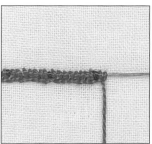

9. Continue working stitches in the same manner.

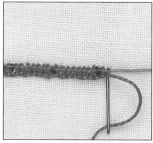

10. To finish, take the needle to the back of the fabric, just over the last loop and outside the shape.

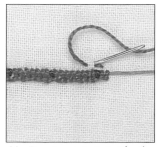

11. Re-emerge just inside the shape and work two tiny back stitches to secure.

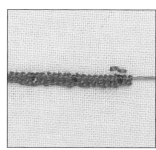

12. Trim the thread close to the back stitches.

- BUTTONHOLE STITCH -

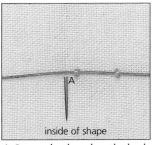 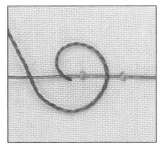 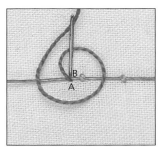 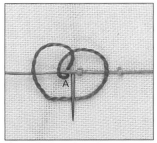

1. Secure the thread on the back of the fabric. Keeping the needle at right angles to the fabric, bring it to the front at A, just inside the wire.

2. Pull the thread through. Loop the thread in a clockwise direction.

3. Take the needle to the back of the fabric at B, just outside the wire and within the loop.

4. Pull the thread part way through. Re-emerge next to A, within the loop.

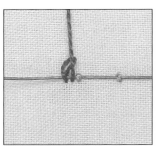 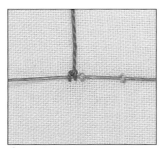 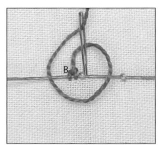 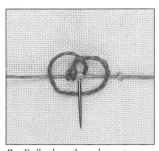

5. Begin to pull the thread towards you and then pull it upwards and away from you. The loop will slip along the thread.

6. Pull firmly until a 'purl' forms on the outer edge of the wire.

7. Loop the thread as before. Take the needle to the back of the fabric next to B, just outside the wire and within the loop.

8. Pull the thread part way through. Re-emerge on the opposite side of the wire within the loop.

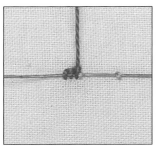 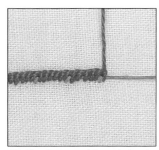 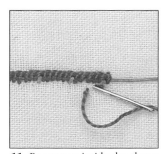 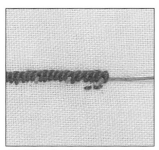

9. Pull the thread firmly as before until a second 'purl' forms.

10. Continue working stitches in the same manner.

11. Re-emerge inside the shape and work two tiny back stitches to secure.

12. Trim the thread close to the back stitches.

- CUTTING OUT WIRED SHAPES -

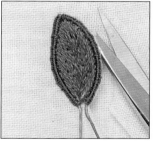 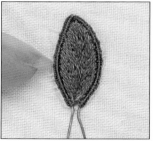  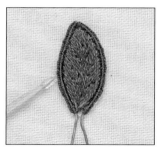

1. Remove the fabric from the hoop. With the right side facing you, carefully cut out the wired shape with small, sharp scissors. Cut as close to the stitching as possible.

2. Rub your fingernail along the cut edge to fluff up any loose threads.

3. Trim the loose threads. Continue to fluff and trim until you are happy with the result.

4. If you accidentally cut a stitch, apply a tiny amount of glue. Allow to dry before completing the cutting out.

- SINKING AND SECURING WIRES -

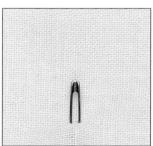   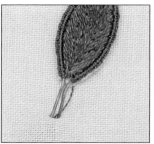

1. Insert a large needle into the fabric at the required position. Push through until the eye is approximately halfway through the fabric.

2. Take the tail or tails of wire from the front to the back of the fabric through the tunnel formed by the needle.

3. Take any tails of thread through the same tunnel.

4. Pull the large needle all the way through and remove.

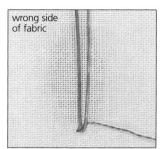 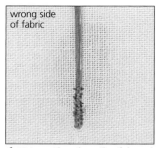 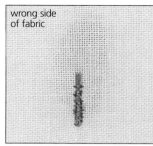 

5. Pull the threads and wire through firmly so the detached shape stands up. Bend the tails of wire into the required position.

6. Using either the tails of thread or a new thread, secure the wire to the fabric with overcast stitch.

7. Trim the tails of wire close to the end of the stitching.

8. Bend the detached shape into the required position.

- CORONNE -

- WORKING A COURONNE AROUND A CYLINDER -

While a cordonnet provides an outer framework for stitching, a couronne provides an inner ring as a framework. They are particularly useful when covering three-dimensional objects (such as beads or marbles) with detached stitches and can also form decorative elements in their own right.

Special ring sticks for working couronnes can be obtained from specialist needlelace shops. The ring stick has various segments at differing diameters.

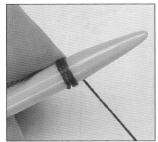

1. Thread a long length of thread into a needle. Wrap it 2 - 3 times around a cylinder of the desired diameter, eg. a knitting needle or pencil.

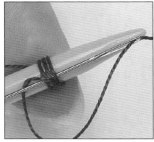

2. Holding the wraps in place, take the needle behind the wraps. Ensure the thread is under the tip of the needle.

3. Pull the thread through until it is firm around the wrapped threads.

4. Again take the needle behind the wrapped threads. Ensure the thread is under the tip of the needle.

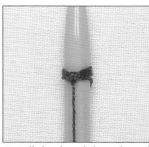

5. Pull the thread through until it is firm around the wrapped threads.

6. Move the ring onto a slightly thinner cylinder to make it easier to work the stitches.

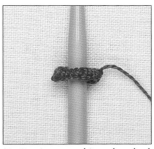

7. Continue working detached blanket stitches around the wrapped threads in the same manner until the ring is tightly packed with stitches.

8. Either end off the thread in the back of the blanket stitches or continue working rounds of detached stitches.

- WORKING A COURONNE ON FABRIC -

1. Draw a circle on the fabric. Work 4 - 6 straight stitches out from the circle ensuring they are evenly spaced.

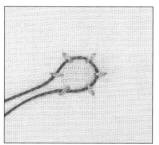

2. Using a new thread, take it behind the stitches around the circle. Do not go through the fabric.

3. Repeat 1 - 2 more times. Again, do not go through the fabric.

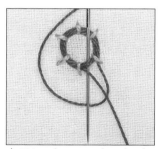

4. Using the same thread, take the needle behind the circle of threads. Ensure the thread is under the tip of the needle.

5. Pull the thread through until it is firm around the circle of threads.

6. Again take the needle behind the circle of threads. Ensure the thread is under the tip of the needle.

7. Pull the thread through until it is firm around the circle of threads. Continue working in the same manner until the circle is tightly packed with stitches.

8. Cut the straight stitches and remove the couronne.

Hints

1. When finished shapes have no background fabric, use thin plastic or tracing paper over a piece of fabric or a needlelace pad for your working background. Couch through both layers. The plastic or paper ensures you do not inadvertently catch any fabric threads into your needlelace stitching.

2. When attaching pieces of needlelace directly onto the background fabric, use matching thread, and small, close stitches.

3. If attaching beads or other objects to needlelace, first back the needlelace with a fine fabric in a matching colour to provide added strength.

- CORDONNET -

- THREAD CORDONNET -

The cordonnet is the foundation or frame on which detached stitches can be worked. It can be made of couched wire, couched thread or stitches such as split back stitch or chain stitch.

If the piece of needlelace is to be completely detached from the fabric, a couched thread or wire needs to be used. The couching stitches are the only stitches that are taken through the fabric. These are cut away after the piece is finished so that the background fabric can be completely removed.

In stumpwork, the detached stitches are often worked over a background fabric that remains as part of the design.

Always ensure the cordonnet is taut. This makes it easier to space stitches evenly and maintain an even tension.

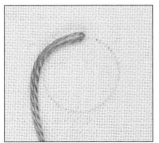

1. Double the thread and begin to lay it on the outline.

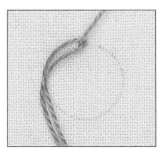

2. Secure the couching thread on the back of the fabric and bring it to the front through the loop of the doubled thread.

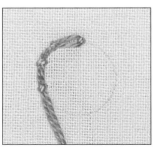

3. Begin couching the doubled thread to the outline, keeping it taut.

4. Continue in the same manner until near the beginning again.

5. Take the tails of doubled thread through the loop.

6. Bend one tail back on itself and couch over it and the previously laid threads.

7. Lay the second tail in the opposite direction and couch over it and the previously laid threads.

8. Take the couching thread to the back of the fabric and secure.

- DETACHED BLANKET STITCH -

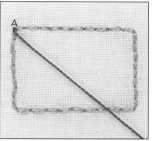

1. Work a framework, using your chosen method around the outer edge of the shape. Secure the thread and bring it to the front at A.

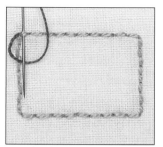

2. Take the needle behind the framework only. Ensure the thread is under the tip of the needle.

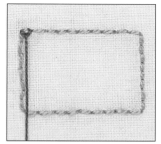

3. Pull the thread through.

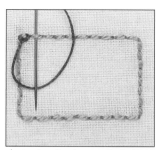

4. Again take the needle behind the framework only. Ensure the thread is under the tip of the needle.

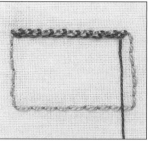

5. Pull the thread through. Continue to the end of the row in the same manner.

6. Slide the needle from right to left under the framework at the side.

7. Pull the thread through. Again, slide the needle from right to left under the framework at the side.

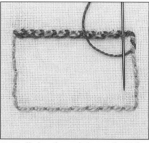

8. Pull the thread through. Take the needle behind the loop of the last stitch of the previous row. Ensure the thread is under the tip of the needle.

9. Pull the thread through.

10. Take the needle behind the loop of the next stitch of the previous row. Ensure the thread is under the tip of the needle.

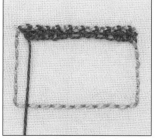

11. Pull the thread through. Continue across the row in the same manner, working a stitch into every loop of the previous row.

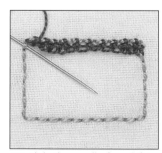

12. Slide the needle from left to right under the framework at the side.

- DETACHED BLANKET STITCH CONTINUED -

13. Pull the thread through. Again, slide the needle from left to right under the framework at the side.

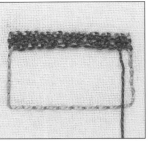

14. Pull the thread through. Work back across the row in the same manner as before.

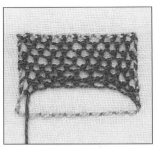

15. Continue working rows until the shape is almost filled.

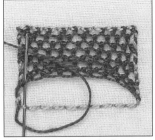

16. When working the last row, take the needle behind the framework as well as the loops of the previous row.

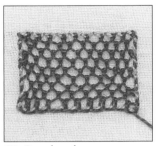

17. Complete the row.

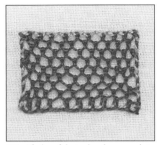

18. If the fabric background is to remain, take the thread to the back of the fabric and secure.

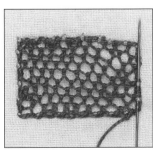

19. If the fabric will be removed, work 1 - 2 tiny back stitches on the underside of the framework and then slide the needle behind the stitching or threads.

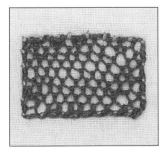

20. Pull the thread through and cut off the excess thread.

Hints

1. When working needlewoven picots and bars, fit in as many rows of weaving as you can. This ensures the picots and bars are firm and makes it easier to twist and manipulate them into the shape you want.

2. Untwist your working thread often to avoid knots and tangles.

3. Detached blanket stitch can be worked in concentric rows around a shape as well as from side to side. You can also create variations by adding extra stitches into the loop of a previous row or by not stitching into some of the loops of a previous row.

4. If you want to avoid joining in a new thread in the middle of a row, don't start a new row unless your thread is at least three times as long as the length of the row.

- CORDED DETACHED BLANKET STITCH -

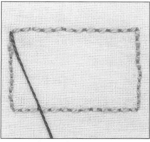

1. Work a framework, using your chosen method, around the outer edge of the shape. Secure the thread and bring it to the front at A.

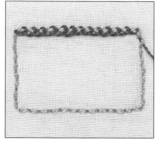

2. Stitch the first row and anchor it at the side, following steps 2 - 7 on page 33.

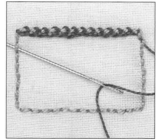

3. Slide the needle from right to left under the framework on the opposite side, forming a long laid thread across the shape.

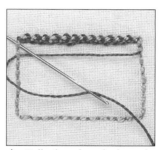

4. Pull the thread through. Again, slide the needle from right to left under the framework at this side.

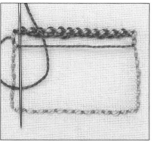

5. Take the needle behind the first loop of the previous row and the laid thread. Ensure the thread is under the tip of the needle.

6. Pull the thread through.

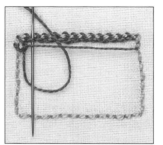

7. Take the needle behind both the loop of the next stitch in the previous row and the laid thread. Ensure the thread is under the tip of the needle.

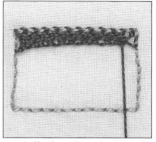

8. Pull the thread through. Continue across the row in the same manner.

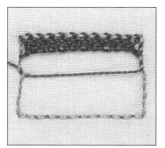

9. Take the thread around the side of the framework in the same manner as before, and then around the framework on the opposite side.

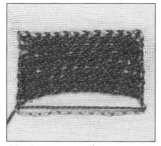

10. Continue working rows in the same manner until the shape is almost filled.

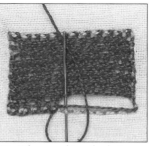

11. When working the last row, take the needle behind the framework as well as the loops of the previous row and the laid thread.

12. Finish off following steps 18 - 20 on page 34.

- N E E D L E W E A V I N G -

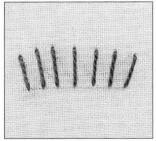

1. Secure the thread on the back of the fabric. Work the required number of straight stitches for the foundation. The stitches can be parallel or fanned.

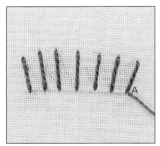

2. Bring the thread to the front at A, very close to the base of the last straight stitch.

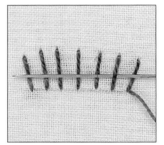

3. Take the needle over the first straight stitch and under the second stitch. The needle does not go through the fabric.

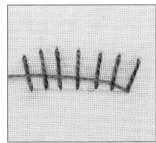

4. Continue weaving over and under to the opposite side.

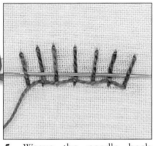

5. Weave the needle back through the straight stitches to the other side. Pack down the stitches of the first row with the needle.

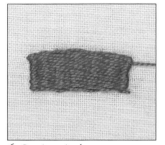

6. Continue in the same manner until the shape is the required height, firmly packing each row of weaving with the needle.

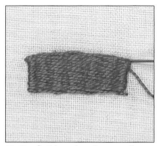

7. To finish, take the needle to the back of the fabric as close as possible to the last used foundation stitch.

8. Pull the thread through and end off on the back of the fabric.

- N E E D L E W E A V I N G - O P E N B A S E P I C O T -

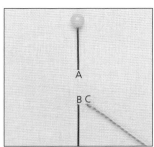

1. Insert a long pin into the fabric from A - B. A - B is the length of the picot. Secure the thread on the back of the fabric and bring it to the front at C.

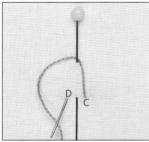

2. Take the thread from right to left behind the head of the pin. Take the needle to the back at D.

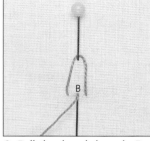

3. Pull the thread through. Re-emerge just to the right of B and pull the thread through.

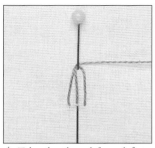

4. Take the thread from left to right behind the head of the pin. Firmly tug the thread to the right.

- NEEDLEWEAVING - OPEN BASE PICOT CONTINUED -

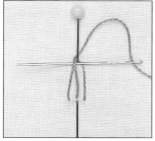

5. Near the top of the pin weave the thread from right to left through the foundation threads - over, under over.

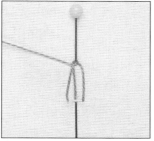

6. Pull the thread through, pulling firmly against the pin.

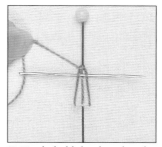

7. Firmly hold the thread to the left. Take the needle from left to right through the foundation stitches - under, over, under.

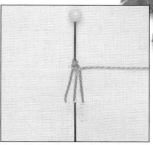

8. Pull the thread through until the loop lies snugly against the first foundation thread.

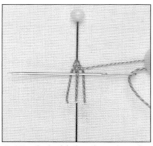

9. Firmly hold the thread to the right. Take the needle from right to left through the foundation stitches - over, under, over.

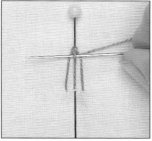

10. Push the needle up towards the top of the picot to pack the threads as tightly as possible.

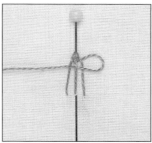

11. Pull the thread almost all the way through.

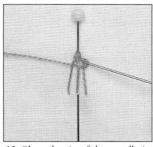

12. Place the tip of the needle in the loop on the right. Keeping tension on the thread with the needle, pull the thread until it lies snugly against the foundation thread.

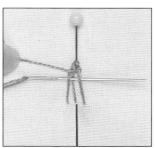

13. Firmly hold the thread to the left. Take the needle from left to right through the foundation stitches - under, over, under.

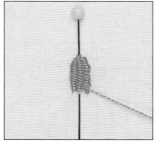

14. Continue weaving the thread back and forth, packing each row with the needle, until the foundation threads are completely covered.

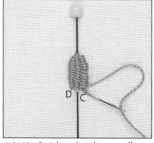

15. To finish, take the needle to the back of the fabric close to D or C, depending on which side you have finished weaving.

16. Pull the thread through and end off on the back of the fabric. Remove the pin.

- N E E D L E W E A V I N G - C L O S E D   B A S E   P I C O T -

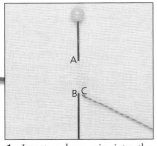

1. Insert a long pin into the fabric from A - B. A - B is the length of the picot. Secure the thread on the back of the fabric and bring it to the front at C.

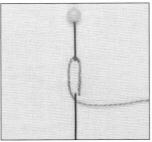

2. Take the thread from right to left behind the head of the pin and then left to right under the tip. Do not pull too tightly.

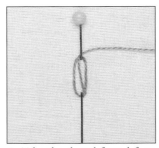

3. Take the thread from left to right behind the head of the pin to form a third foundation stitch.

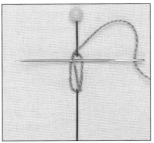

4. Near the top of the pin, weave the needle from right to left through the foundation threads - over, under, over.

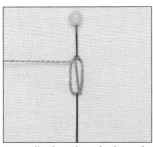

5. Pull the thread through, pulling firmly against the pin.

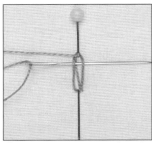

6. Firmly hold the thread to the left. Take the needle from left to right through the foundation stitches - under, over, under.

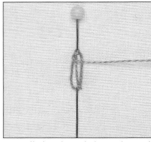

7. Pull the thread through until the loop lies snugly against the foundation thread.

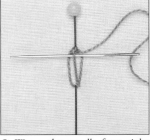

8. Weave the needle from right to left through the foundation threads - over, under, over. Push the needle up towards the top of the picot to pack the threads close together.

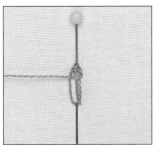

9. Pull the thread through until the loop lies snugly against the foundation thread.

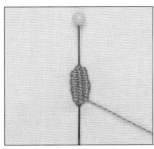

10. Continue weaving the thread back and forth, packing each row with the needle, until the foundation threads are completely covered.

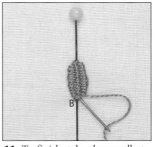

11. To finish, take the needle to the back of the fabric close to B.

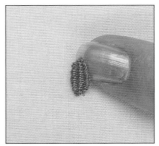

12. Pull the thread through and end off on the back of the fabric. Remove the pin.

- NEEDLEWEAVING - BAR -

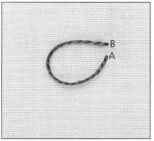

1. Secure the thread on the back of the fabric. Bring it to the front at A and take it to the back at B, leaving a loop on the front.

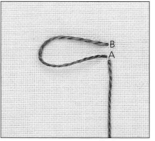

2. Re-emerge just below A, taking care not to pull the loop through.

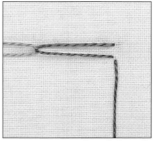

3. Pass a waste thread through the loop. Hold it taut slightly above the fabric while you work the bar.

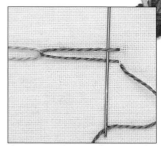

4. Weave the needle over the lower thread of the loop and under the upper thread. Do not go through the fabric.

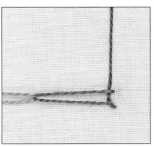

5. Firmly pull the thread through.

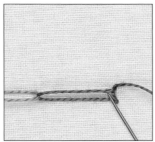

6. Push the thread down onto the fabric with the tip of the needle.

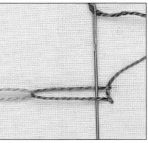

7. Weave the needle over the upper thread and under the lower thread. Do not go through the fabric.

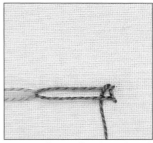

8. Firmly pull the thread through.

9. Push the woven thread down the loop so it lies snugly against the first woven thread.

10. Continue in the same manner until the loop is completely filled and the woven threads are firmly packed.

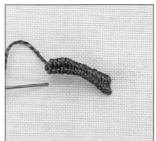

11. Remove the waste thread. To finish, take the needle to the back of the fabric at the required position.

12. Pull the thread through and end off on the back of the fabric.

- ATTACHING A BEAD -

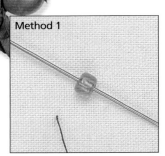

Method 1

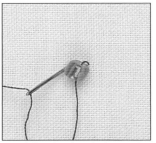

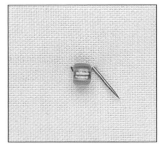

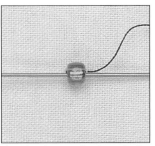

1. Secure the thread on the back of the fabric and bring it to the front. Thread the bead onto the needle.

2. Slide the bead down the thread to the fabric. Take the needle to the back at the end of the bead.

3. Pull the thread through. Re-emerge at the other end of the bead.

4. Take the needle through the bead again.

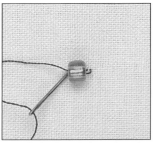

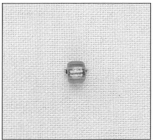

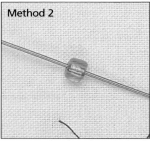

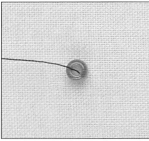

5. Pull the thread through. Take the needle to the back of the fabric at the end of the bead.

6. Pull the thread through. End off on the back of the fabric.

Method 2

1. Secure the thread on the back of the fabric and bring it to the front. Thread the bead onto the needle.

2. Slide the bead down the thread to the fabric. Hold the bead on the fabric so the hole is uppermost.

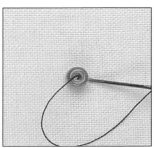

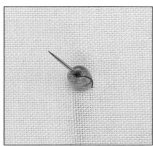

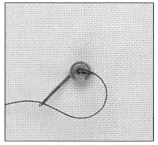

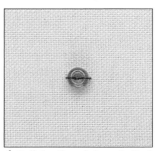

3. Take the needle to the back of the fabric on one side of the bead.

4. Pull the thread through. Bring the needle up through the bead again.

5. Pull the thread through. Take the needle to the back of the fabric on the other side of the bead.

6. Pull the thread through. End off on the back of the fabric.

- ATTACHING A PAIR OF BEADS -

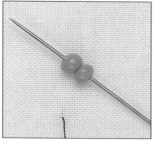

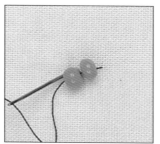

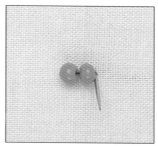

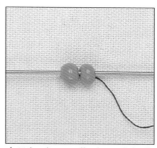

1. Secure the thread on the back of the fabric and bring it to the front. Thread two beads onto the needle.

2. Slide the beads down the thread to the fabric. Take the needle to the back at the end of the second bead.

3. Pull the thread through. Re-emerge at the end of the first bead.

4. Take the needle through both beads again.

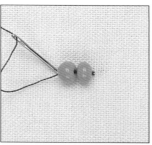

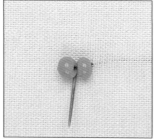

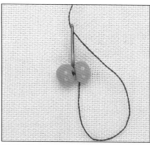

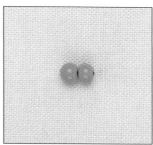

5. Pull the thread through. Take the needle to the back of the fabric at the end of the second bead.

6. Pull the thread through. Bring the needle to the front between the two beads.

7. Pull the thread through. Take the needle to the back of the fabric just over the threads between the beads.

8. Pull the thread through. Secure the thread on the back of the fabric.

- ATTACHING A BEAD TO THE END OF A BEAD -

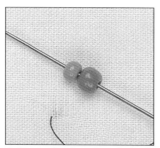

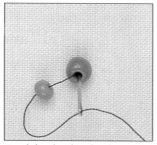

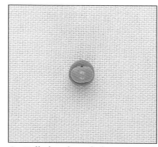

1. Secure the thread on the back of the fabric and bring it to the front. Thread two beads onto the needle.

2. Slide the beads down the thread to the fabric. Take the needle back through the first bead only and through the fabric.

3. Pull the thread through and end off on the back of the fabric.

- ATTACHING A STRING OF BEADS -

Method 1

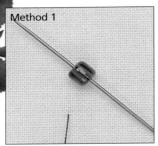

1. Secure the thread on the back of the fabric and bring it to the front. Thread a bead onto the needle.

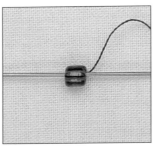

2. Attach the bead following steps 2 - 4 of method 1 on page 40.

3. Pull the thread through. Thread a second bead onto the needle. Take the needle to the back of the fabric at the end of the bead.

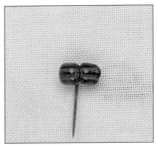

4. Pull the thread through. Re-emerge between the two beads.

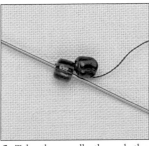

5. Take the needle through the second bead again.

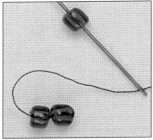

6. Pull the thread through. Thread a third bead onto the needle.

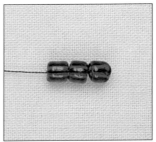

7. Secure the bead to the fabric in the same manner as before.

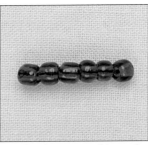

8. Continue attaching the required number of beads in the same manner. After attaching the last bead, take the thread to the back of the fabric and secure.

Method 2

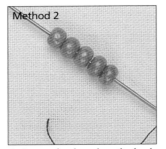

1. Secure the thread on the back of the fabric and bring it to the front. Thread the required number of beads onto the needle.

2. Slide the beads down the thread. Take the needle to the back of the fabric at the required position.

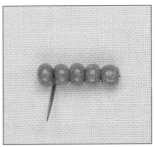

3. Pull the thread through. Bring the needle to the front between the last two beads.

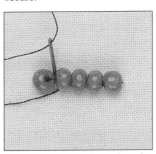

4. Pull the thread through. Take the needle to the back of the fabric just over the thread between the two beads.

- ATTACHING A STRING OF BEADS CONTINUED -

5. Pull the thread through. Re-emerge between the next two beads.

6. Pull the thread through. Take it to the back of the fabric just over the thread between the two beads.

7. Pull the thread through. Continue couching the thread between the beads in the same manner.

8. To finish, secure the thread on the back of the fabric after the last couching stitch.

- ATTACHING A CIRCLE OF BEADS -

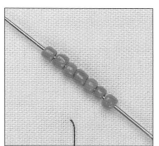

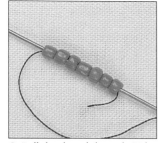

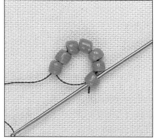

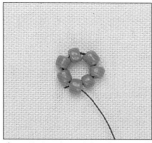

1. Secure the thread on the back of the fabric and bring it to the front. Thread the required number of beads onto the needle.

2. Pull the thread through. Take the needle through all beads in the same order that they were first threaded onto the needle.

3. Pull the thread through. Take the needle through the first bead.

4. Pull the thread firmly to pull the beads into a circle.

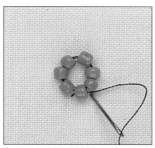

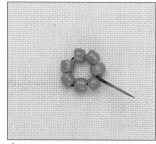

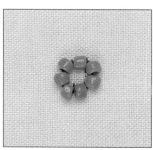

5. Position the circle on the fabric. Take the needle to the back of the fabric between the first and second beads.

6. Pull the thread through. Re-emerge between the second and third beads.

7. Couch the beads to the fabric following steps 4 - 7 of method 2 on pages 42 - 43.

8. To finish, secure the thread on the back of the fabric after the last couching stitch.

- CHIPPING -

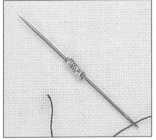

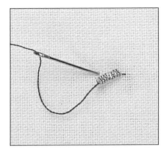

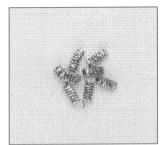

1. Using sharp scissors (not your fabric or embroidery scissors), cut the purl into short lengths. Cut over a pad of velvet. This will prevent the chips from rolling away.

2. Secure the thread on the back of the fabric and bring it to the front. Thread a chip onto the needle, taking care not to stretch it.

3. Slide the chip down the thread to the fabric. Take the needle to the back at the end of the chip.

4. Continue attaching chips in the same manner. Varying the angles that the chips lie gives a more spectacular appearance as they catch the light.

- COVERING A BEAD - WRAPPING -

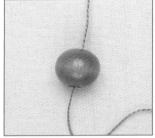

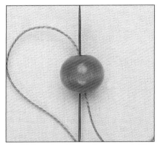

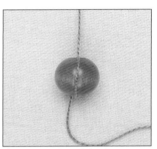

1. If necessary, slightly enlarge the hole of the bead by scraping it out with a small round file or small tube of sandpaper.

2. Using a long thread, take it through the bead. Leave a tail of at least 5cm (2") to hold onto.

3. Take the thread around the bead and through the hole in the same direction as before.

4. Pull the thread firmly.

5. Continue taking the thread through the hole (always in the same direction) and pulling firmly until the bead is completely covered.

6. Take the needle back through the bead. Ensure it is in a different place from where it emerged and catch it through the threads inside the bead.

7. Pull the thread through.

8. Attach the bead to the fabric with the tails of thread.

- COVERING A BEAD - NEEDLELACE -

1. Make a couronne around a cylinder following the instructions on page 30. Lightly glue to the top of the bead.

2. Alternatively, wrap the bead several times following the instructions on page 44. Ensure the wraps are evenly spaced.

3. At the top of the bead, take the thread behind the wrapping threads for 2 - 3 rounds to form a circle of thread.

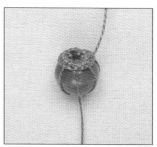

4. Work detached blanket stitch over the circle of threads to form the couronne.

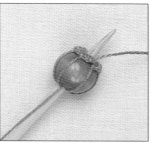

5. Place a skewer or similar through the base of the bead as a temporary handle.

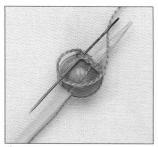

6. Begin working detached blanket stitch into the couronne.

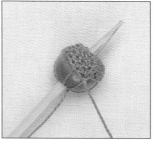

7. Continue working rounds of detached blanket stitch, increasing and decreasing the number of stitches in each round to fit the shape of the bead.

Hints

1. Use a beading thread such as Nymo for attaching beads. Alternatively, use machine sewing thread and pass it through some beeswax to add strength.

8. Remove the skewer before working the last row.

9. Take the working thread (and any others, depending on the method used for the couronne) through the hole in the bead.

10. Attach the bead to the fabric with the tails of thread.

2. Always use a needle with a slender shaft and small eye such as a beading or straw needle. If you are having difficulty taking the needle through a bead, don't force it as you may crack the bead. Change to a smaller needle.

by Anna Scott

- MAGIC MUSHROOMS -

THIS DESIGN USES

Back stitch, Beading, Blanket stitch, Bullion knot

Corded detached blanket stitch, Couching, Detached chain

Fly stitch, Long and short stitch, Needlewoven bar, Overcast stitch

Padded satin stitch, Raised stem stitch, Satin stitch, Single feather stitch

Split stitch, Stab stitch, Stem stitch, Straight stitch

Whipped chain stitch, Wirework, Whipping

MATERIALS

Threads, beads and needles

DMC stranded cotton
A = ecru
B = 830 dark golden olive
C = 3011 dark khaki green
D = 3012 medium khaki green

DMC no. 5 perlé cotton
E = 830 dark golden olive

Anchor stranded cotton
F = 11 bright coral
G = 13 dark coral
H = 20 dark ruby
I = 873 very dark antique violet

Madeira stranded silk
J = 1314 pine green
K = 1409 very light avocado green
L = 1508 olive green
M = 2008 mahogany
N = 2014 cream
O = 2114 medium hazelnut brown
P = 2400 black

Au Ver à Soie, Soie d'Alger
Q = 3424 medium silver green
R = 4635 dark antique mauve

Needlepaints stranded cotton
S = 2006 French navy

DMC stranded metallic thread
T = 5283 silver

Mill Hill glass seed beads
U = 00367 garnet

Delica Beads
V = DBR323 matte metallic purple iris

No. 8 straw (milliner's) needle

No. 9 crewel needle

No. 10 crewel needle

No. 10 beading needle

No. 24 tapestry needle

Long darner

Supplies

Main fabric

Backing fabric

Quilter's muslin
15cm x 30cm wide (6" x 12")

Green homespun 15cm (6") square

Fusible webbing
5cm x 10cm wide (2" x 4")

White felt 5cm (2") square

Red felt 5cm (2") square

30cm (12") no. 28 gauge uncovered wire

Embroidery hoop
10cm (4") diameter

Embroidery hoop
20cm (8") diameter

ORDER OF WORK

Use the long darner when sinking the wires, the beading needle for attaching the beads, the straw needle for working the bullion knots, and the tapestry needle for laying threads, whipping and needleweaving. The no. 10 crewel needle is used when stitching with one strand of thread and the no. 9 crewel needle when stitching with more than one strand.

Transfer the design using your chosen method and mount the main fabric in the larger hoop.

Leaves on main fabric

Upper leaves on left hand side

Embroider the centre vein of both leaves with whipped chain stitch. Beginning at the tip of the leaf on the right, fill each half of the upper segment with satin stitch. Begin the remaining segments with a detached chain at the tip and then fill in with fly stitches.

Outline the leaf on the left with split stitch. Pad each half with straight stitches parallel to the centre vein. Using a different thread colour for each half, cover the padding and split stitch with satin stitch.

Upper leaves on right hand side

Using different thread colours, stitch this pair of leaves in the same manner as those on the left.

Lower leaves on right hand side

Stitch the leaf on the right in the same manner as the previous padded satin stitched leaves. For the leaf on the left, work whipped chain stitch for the centre vein and then fill in each half of the leaf with closely worked rows of stem stitch. Add single feather stitch markings over the stem stitching.

Lower leaf in the centre

This leaf is embroidered after the stems are complete. Outline the lower half with split stitch. Pad each half of the leaf with straight stitches

that are roughly parallel to the stem. Fill the lower half with blanket stitch, keeping the purls of the stitches along the middle. Avoid working the stitches too firmly so the purls remain raised.

Cover the upper half in the same manner, keeping the purls along the outer edge.

Detached leaves

Place the green homespun in the smaller hoop and transfer the leaf shapes. Cut five pieces of wire, each 6cm (2 3/8") long. Each leaf is worked in the same manner but different thread colours are used.

Couch a wire to the centre vein of one leaf. Work overcast stitch along the centre vein, covering the wire. Outline the leaf with split stitch. Pad each half of the leaf with straight stitches parallel to the centre vein. Using a different thread colour for each half, cover the split stitch with blanket stitch and fill in the leaf with satin stitch. When working the satin stitch, bring the needle to the front at the inside edge of the blanket stitch, sharing the same holes in the fabric. Angle the needle under the centre vein when taking it to the back of the fabric. Stitch the remaining leaves in the same manner. Carefully cut out the leaves and set them aside.

Stems

Begin the three main stems with two rows of blanket stitch to create thorns. Work a row on each side of the design lines. Leave a space where the stem on the right goes over the top of the middle stem.

Lay two lengths of perlé cotton along the design line for the left stem and couch in place. Using blended threads, work overcast stitch over the laid threads. Embroider the middle stem in the same manner. Where the stem crosses the leaf, whip the laid threads together rather than overcasting. To work the right stem, lay the lengths of perlé cotton over the middle stem and work overcast stitch until approximately 3mm (1/8") from the middle stem. Whip the laid threads for approximately 1cm (3/8") and then continue to the end of the stem with overcast stitch.

Work a bullion knot for each short blackberry stem. Allow extra wraps so the stems curve.

Spider

Stitch the body with padded satin stitch and the legs with back stitch. Form the web, work a long straight stitch between the tips of the two upper leaves and then a fly stitch, which ends at the top of the spider.

Toadstools

Small toadstool

Fill the stem with closely worked rows of stem stitch and the spots with padded satin stitch. Outline the cap with stem stitch. Using the lighter shade at the top and grading to the darker shade near the lower edge, fill the cap with long and short stitch.

Large toadstool

Transfer the padding shapes for the stem to the fusible webbing. Fuse to the white felt and cut out. Centre the smaller piece of padding within the outline on the main fabric and attach with stab stitches. Centre the larger piece over the first and attach in the same manner.

Work a foundation of horizontal straight stitches approximately 3mm (1/8") apart over the padding. Beginning at the centre, embroider the stem with raised stem stitch.

Transfer the padding shapes for the cap to the fusible web. Fuse to the red felt and cut out. Attach the two pieces in the same manner as the stem padding.

Cut the quilter's muslin into two 15cm (6") squares. Transfer the cap design to the fabric and mount in the smaller hoop. Embroider the cap in the same manner as the cap for the smaller toadstool.

Work a row of running stitch around the cap 3mm (1/8") away from the embroidery. Cut out leaving a 6mm (1/4") seam allowance. Turn the seam allowance under, gathering it in by pulling up the running stitches. Secure it at intervals to hold it in place. Work blanket stitch along the lower edge, taking the stitches over the folded edge of the fabric.

Position the cap over the padding on the main fabric and stitch around all sides, leaving a 2cm (3/4") opening along the lower edge.

Blackberries

Transfer the berry shapes to the remaining square of quilter's muslin and mount in the smaller hoop.

Cover each shape with diagonal rows of corded detached blanket stitch. Work bullion knots, of varying lengths, over the corded blanket stitch. Gradually shade the knots from dark at the upper edges of the berries to light at the lower edges. Randomly attach three beads of each colour between the bullion knots.

Work a row of running stitch around each berry 3mm (1/8") away from the embroidery. Cut out each one leaving a 5mm (3/16") seam allowance. Pull up the running stitches to gather. Secure each berry to the fabric with tiny stab stitches.

At the top of each berry, work three needlewoven bars for sepals.

Applying the detached leaves

Using the long darner, sink the wires of the leaves. On the wrong side, bend each wire behind its leaf and secure. Trim excess wire and gently manipulate the leaves to shape them.

EMBROIDERY KEY

All embroidery is worked with one strand of thread unless otherwise specified.

Leaves on main fabric

Upper leaves on left

Centre veins = C and K
(whipped chain stitch)

Left leaf = L and Q
(split stitch, padded satin stitch)

Right leaf = L and Q (detached chain, fly stitch, satin stitch)

Upper leaves on right

Centre vein of left leaf = C and O (whipped chain stitch)

Left leaf = J and L (detached chain, fly stitch, satin stitch)

Centre vein of right leaf = C and K (whipped chain stitch)

Right leaf = L and Q
(split stitch, padded satin stitch)

Lower leaves on right

Centre veins = C and O (whipped chain stitch)

Left leaf = J and L (stem stitch)

Marking on leaf = B and C (single feather stitch)

Right leaf = J and L
(split stitch, padded satin stitch)

Lower leaf in the centre

Outline = O (split stitch)

Padding = E
(2 strands, straight stitch)

Leaf = L and O (blanket stitch)

Detached leaves

Upper left leaf

Outline = L (split stitch)

Centre vein = K
(couching, overcast stitch)

Leaf = D and L (blanket stitch, padded satin stitch)

Lower left leaf

Outline = L (split stitch)

Centre vein = O
(couching, overcast stitch)

Leaf = L and Q
(blanket stitch, padded satin stitch)

Upper right leaf

Outline = L (split stitch)

Centre vein = K
(couching, overcast stitch)

Leaf = L and Q
(blanket stitch, padded satin stitch)

Lower two leaves on right

Outline = L (split stitch)

Centre vein = O
(couching, overcast stitch)

Leaf = J and L (blanket stitch, padded satin stitch)

Stems

Main stems

Thorns = B (blanket stitch)

Stems = E (2 strands, laid thread), M blended with O
(1 strand of each, couching, whipping, overcast stitch)

Small stems = M blended with O
(1 strand of each, bullion knot, 12 - 18 wraps)

Toadstools

Small toadstool

Stem = A blended with N
(1 strand of each, stem stitch)

Spots = A (padded satin stitch)

Cap outline = G
(2 strands, stem stitch)

Cap filling = F blended with G, G blended with H, G and H
(1 strand of each or 2 strands, long and short stitch)

Large toadstool

Stem = A blended with N (1 strand of each, raised stem stitch)

Spots = A (padded satin stitch)

Cap outline = G
(2 strands, stem stitch)

Cap filling = F blended with G, G blended with H, G and H
(1 strand of each or 2 strands, long and short stitch)

Lower edge of cap = H
(2 strands, blanket stitch)

Blackberries

Berry = S
(corded detached blanket stitch)

Seeds = I blended with R, I blended with S, I and S (1 strand of each or 2 strands, bullion knot, 7 - 24 wraps), U and V (beading)

Sepals = C blended with K, and C blended with L (1 strand of each, needlewoven bar)

Spider

Body = P (padded satin stitch)

Legs = P (back stitch)

Web = T (straight stitch, fly stitch)

- NATURE'S DINER -

MATERIALS

Threads, beads and needles

DMC stranded cotton
A = 115 variegated ruby
B = 740 tangerine
C = 907 light parrot green
D = 3345 dark hunter green
E = 3346 hunter green

DMC no.5 perlé cotton
F = 3345 dark hunter green

DMC soft tapestry cotton
G = 2437 avocado green

Rajmahal artificial silk
H = 29 charcoal
I = 144 persimmon

Splendour stranded silk
J = S802 white

Madeira metallic thread
K = 5014 black-gold

Mill Hill antique glass beads
L = 03055 bay leaf

Mill Hill petite glass beads
M = 40374 rainbow

No. 3 straw (milliner's) needle
No. 7 crewel needle
No. 10 crewel needle
No. 26 tapestry needle
Long darner

THIS DESIGN USES

Back stitch, Beading, Blanket stitch, Bullion knot, Couching, Detached blanket stitch
Detached chain, French knot, Granitos, Needlewoven bar, Overcast stitch, Padded satin stitch
Raised stem stitch, Split back stitch, Straight stitch, Whipped chain stitch, Wirework, Wrapping

Supplies

Main fabric

Backing fabric

Quilter's muslin 15cm (6") square

Red felt 5cm (2") square

Fusible webbing 5cm (2") square

60cm (24") no. 30 gauge green covered wire

45cm (18") no. 30 gauge white covered wire

Embroidery hoop 10cm (4") diameter

Embroidery hoop 15cm (6") diameter

ORDER OF WORK

Use the long darner when laying threads and sinking wires, the straw needle for working the bullion knots and the tapestry needle for working the raised stem stitch and whipping. The no. 10 crewel needle is used for all other embroidery worked with one strand of thread and for attaching the beads. The no. 7 crewel needle is used for all other embroidery worked with more than one strand of thread.

Transfer the design using your chosen method and mount the main fabric in the larger hoop.

Strawberry

Stems

Embroider all stems with whipped chain stitch, using three strands of thread for the main stem and two strands for the smaller stems.

Berry

Trace the shapes for the berry padding onto the right side of the fusible webbing. Fuse to the felt and cut out. Centre the smaller piece of felt inside the berry outline. Attach with several tiny stab stitches. Centre the larger piece of felt over the first and attach in the same manner.

Outline the edge of the felt with small back stitches. Using the same thread and beginning at the top, cover the felt with rows of detached blanket stitch. Again beginning at the top, embroider bullion knots over the entire berry. Vary the angle of the knots as you work towards the lower edge. Randomly attach beads among the knots for seeds.

Stitch three needlewoven bars for the sepals, anchoring them within the berry.

Detached leaves

Place the quilter's muslin in the smaller hoop and transfer six leaf shapes. Cut the green covered wire into six pieces, each 10cm (4") long.

Beginning at the tip of one leaf, couch a wire in place along the vein. Cover the wire with overcast stitch for the length of the centre vein. Shape the wire to fit the outline and couch in place *(diag 1)*. Embroider closely packed blanket stitches over the wire to completely cover it and then a row of split back stitch just inside the blanket stitch edging. Work straight stitches in each half of the leaf for padding and then cover with satin stitch, enclosing the split back stitch outline. Using the lighter shade of green thread, add 2 - 3 straight stitches to each half for markings. Repeat for the remaining leaves.

Diag 1

Carefully cut out the leaves and set them aside.

Flower

Embroider the petals on the main fabric with blanket stitch.

Transfer six petal shapes onto tracing paper. Pin the paper to a needlelace pad. Cut the white covered wire into six pieces, each 7.5cm (3") long.

Couch one wire around a petal shape, leaving two tails of wire extending. Cover the wire with closely packed blanket stitches, keeping the purls to the inside of the wire. Fill the petal with rows of detached blanket stitch. Work the remaining petals in the same manner.

Carefully cut away the couching stitches from the petals and set them aside.

Bee

Work a granitos of three horizontal straight stitches for the body. Add the stripes with straight stitches and the wings with detached chains.

Caterpillar

Couch down three lengths of soft tapestry cotton for padding, placing the couching stitches approximately 3mm (1/8") apart. Using the couching stitches as foundation stitches, cover the padding with raised stem stitch. Embroider the centre row with the persimmon thread and the remaining rows with the green thread. Add French knots below the body for legs and two straight stitches for the antennae. Attach a bead for the head.

Applying the detached pieces

Leaves

Bind the wires of three leaves together for approximately 6mm (1/4") from the base of the leaves. Sink the wires together and secure them on the back of the fabric. Bind and attach the three remaining leaves in the same manner. Trim the excess wire.

Flower

Sink the wire of each petal just inside the petals embroidered on the main fabric, positioning them evenly around the centre. Secure the wires on the back of the fabric and trim the excess wire. Fill the centre with closely packed French knots.

Watermark, *Inspirations* issue 17

EMBROIDERY KEY

All embroidery is worked with one strand of thread unless otherwise specified.

Strawberry

Berry

Outline = K (back stitch)

Fruit = K (detached blanket stitch), A (2 strands, bullion knot, 12 wraps)

Seeds = L (beading)

Sepals = F (needlewoven bar)

Flower

Petals on main fabric = J (blanket stitch)

Outlines of detached petals = J (couching, blanket stitch)

Filling of detached petals = J (detached blanket stitch)

Centre = C blended with J (1 strand of each, French knot, 1 wrap)

Detached leaves

Centre vein = E (couching, overcast stitch)

Outline = D (couching, split back stitch, blanket stitch)

Filling = D (padded satin stitch)

Markings = E (straight stitch)

Stems = D (wrapping)

Stems

Main stem = D (3 strands, whipped chain stitch)

Small stems = D (2 strands, whipped chain stitch)

Bee

Body = I (6 strands, granitos)

Stripes = H (6 strands, straight stitch)

Wings = K (detached chain)

Caterpillar

Padding = G (laid thread), C (couching)

Body = B and C (2 strands, raised stem stitch)

Head = M (beading)

Antennae = K (straight stitch)

Legs = C (French knot, 1 wrap)

by Helen Hardman

- A N G E L -

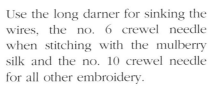

THIS DESIGN USES

Back stitch, Blanket stitch

Chain stitch, Couching

Ghiordes knot

Long and short stitch

Overcast stitch, Padded satin stitch

Satin stitch, Split stitch

Straight stitch, Wirework

MATERIALS

Threads and needles

DMC stranded cotton

A = blanc

B = 310 black

C = 712 cream

D = 801 dark coffee brown

E = 813 light blue

F = 838 dark chocolate

G = 842 very light beige

H = 902 maroon

I = 3033 very light putty groundings

Au Ver à Soie, Soie d'Alger

J = 611 very light copper

K = 612 light copper

L = 4646 very dark plum

Kaalund Yarns hand-dyed mulberry silk

M = S521 wine

N = S538 hydrangea

Kreinik metallic cord

O = 001C silver

No. 6 crewel needle

No. 10 crewel needle

Long darner

Supplies

Main fabric

Backing fabric

Lightweight non-fusible interfacing 30cm x 60cm wide (12" x 24")

20cm (8") no. 28 gauge uncovered wire

Small amount of polyester fibre-fill

2 x embroidery hoops 15cm (6") diameter

ORDER OF WORK

Use the long darner for sinking the wires, the no. 6 crewel needle when stitching with the mulberry silk and the no. 10 crewel needle for all other embroidery.

Mount the main fabric into a hoop and transfer the design using your chosen method.

Cat

Main fabric

Outline the back leg with split stitch. Work a layer of satin stitch across the back paw within the outline. Embroider a second layer of satin stitches that cover the outline and run in the opposite direction to the previous layer. Fill the leg with long and short stitch, using the photograph as a guide to colour placement.

Work split stitch along the tail outline. Beginning at the base, fill the tail with closely packed ghiordes knots. Blend the thread colours from the lightest shade at the base to the darkest shade

approximately one third of the way up the tail.

Slip

Cut the interfacing into two 30cm (12") squares. Place the two pieces together and mount them into a hoop. The two pieces will be treated as one from now on. Transfer the design using your chosen method.

Embroider all outlines, except for the ears, with split stitch. Cut the wire in half. Shape one piece to fit the left ear outline. Position the wire onto the ear, taking the ends to the back of the fabric. Couch the wire in place and secure the ends on the back of the fabric behind the head. Overcast the wire to the fabric and then work long and short stitch within the outline, working from the tip to the base of the ear. Fashion the remaining ear in the same manner.

Stitch the paws in the same manner as the back paw on the main fabric. Add straight stitches over the padded satin stitch for the claws.

Fill the legs with long and short stitch, grading from the darkest shade of brown at the top of the paws to the lightest shade near the body.

Outline the nose, eyes and mouth next. Fill the eyes with satin stitch, using the black thread for the centre of each eye and the blue thread on the sides. Stitch a layer of satin stitch across the nose within the outline. Embroider a second layer of satin stitch that covers the outline and lies in the opposite direction to the previous layer.

Work rows of chain stitch close together on the muzzle for padding. Cover the head and face with long and short stitch following the diagram for the direction of your stitches *(diag 1)*.

Diag 1

Beginning near the back leg, fill the body with closely packed ghiordes knots. Use the photograph as a guide to the shading. Carefully cut the loops and brush the threads. Continue brushing and trimming until the body is soft and fluffy. The fur should be approximately 6mm (1/4") long.

Work the chest in the same manner as the body, starting at the top of the front legs. Continue working ghiordes knots around the face. Carefully cut and brush the thread as before, leaving a ruff across the chest. Cut the knots along the top of the head quite short.

Using the silver metallic thread, work ghiordes knots, with loops approximately 2cm (3/4") long, for the whiskers and eyebrows.

Remove the fabric from the hoop. Leaving a 6mm (1/4") seam allowance beyond the embroidery, cut out the cat. Around the ears, cut as close as possible to the wire

without cutting the stitching. Clip the curves and finger press the seam allowance to the wrong side. Tack the seam allowance in place, taking care to ensure the stitches do not show on the right side.

Position the slip on the main fabric. Beginning with the legs, then back, chest and head, attach the slip to the main fabric. To shape the cat, insert small pieces of polyester fibre-fill as you go.

Fallen leaves and grass

Beginning at the base of one leaf, work blanket stitches from the centre vein to the outer edge along one side. Fan the stitches around the tip and continue along the second side to the base. Add a row of stem stitch for the stem and vein. Work all remaining leaves in the same manner.

To finish, embroider horizontal straight stitches between the leaves and the cat's paws.

EMBROIDERY KEY

All embroidery is worked with one strand of thread unless otherwise specified.

Cat
Ear outlines = F
(couching, overcast stitch)

Ears = F (long and short stitch)

Muzzle padding = F (chain stitch)

Face = D and F
(long and short stitch)

Eye outlines = B (back stitch)

Eyes = B and E (satin stitch)

Nose = B
(split stitch, padded satin stitch)

Mouth = B (back stitch)

Whiskers and eyebrows = O
(2 strands, ghiordes knot)

Body, head and chest outlines
= C (split stitch)

Body = C and G
(2 strands, ghiordes knot)

Head and chest = C (long and short stitch), C and G (2 strands, ghiordes knot)

Front legs = F (split stitch), D, F and G (long and short stitch)

Back legs = F (split stitch), F and G (long and short stitch)

Paws = A
(split stitch, padded satin stitch)

Claws = I (straight stitch)

Tail = F (split stitch), D, F and G (2 strands, ghiordes knot)

Fallen leaves and grass
Grass = N (straight stitch)

Leaf stems and veins = H, J, K, L and M (stem stitch)

Leaves = H, J, K, L and M
(blanket stitch)

by Wendy Innes

- WILD ROSE GARLAND -

THIS DESIGN USES

Back stitch, Beading, Blanket stitch, Couching, Fly stitch, French knot, Ghiordes knot
Long and short stitch, Overcast stitch, Padded satin stitch, Pistil stitch, Satin stitch, Single feather stitch
Split back stitch, Straight stitch, Whipped chain stitch, Wirework

MATERIALS

Threads, beads and needles

DMC stranded cotton

A = ecru
B = 310 black
C = 498 medium garnet
D = 676 light old gold
E = 729 medium old gold
F = 762 very light pearl grey
G = 844 ultra dark beaver grey
H = 895 very dark hunter green
I = 3047 light yellow-beige
J = 3347 medium yellow-green
K = 3608 light fuchsia
L = 3609 very light fuchsia
M = 3820 dark straw

Splendour stranded silk thread
N = S846 pale antique mauve

Kreinik blending filament
O = 032 pearl

Mill Hill glass seed beads
P = 00374 rainbow

No. 10 crewel needle
No. 10 beading needle
No. 18 chenille needle

Supplies

Main fabric

Backing Fabric

White broadcloth 15cm (6") square

White organza 15cm (6") square

80cm (31 1/2") no. 28 gauge
uncovered wire

Embroidery hoop
15cm (6") diameter

Embroidery hoop
10cm (4") diameter

ORDER OF WORK

Use the chenille needle when sinking wires, the beading needle for attaching the beads and the crewel needle for all other embroidery.

Transfer the design using your chosen method and mount the main fabric in the larger hoop.

Garland

Stem and leaves

Embroider the chain stitch stems with the lighter green thread and whip with the darker green thread.

Outline each leaf with split back stitch. Fill each leaf half with satin stitch, covering the split back stitch outline. Beginning at the tip for both sides, work single feather stitch along each side for the leaf serrations. Add a single straight stitch for the centre vein. Stitch all the remaining leaves in the same manner.

Ladybird

Stitch the wings with padded satin stitch and then the head with satin stitch. Work a straight stitch down the centre and add a French knot spot to each wing.

Wild rose

Centre

Fill the centre of the rose with closely packed ghiordes knots. Cut the loops to approximately 3mm (1/8") and comb until fluffy. Trim to form a small mound.

Detached petals

Place the white broadcloth in the smaller hoop and transfer the petal shapes. Cut five pieces of wire, each 12cm (4 3/4") long.

Beginning and ending at the base of one petal, couch a length of wire in place around the shape. Work blanket stitch over the wire, keeping the purls to the outside. Fill the petal with long and short stitch, using the darkest shade of pink on the outer edge and grading to the lightest shade at the base of the petal. Stitch the remaining four petals in the same manner.

Carefully cut out each petal.

Applying the detached petals

Using the chenille needle, sink the wires of the petals at the marked positions. Secure the wires on the back of the fabric and trim excess wire.

Bee

The bee is stitched onto the detached rose petals.

Detached wings

Place the white organza in the smaller hoop and transfer the wing shapes. Cut two pieces of wire, each 10cm (4") long.

Beginning and ending at the base of one wing, couch a length of wire in place around the shape. Overcast the wire to the fabric. Embroider a single fly stitch with a long anchoring stitch for the markings. Repeat for the second wing. Carefully cut out the wings and set them aside.

Body

Beginning at the tail end, fill the body with rows of ghiordes knots. Stitch three rows with the black and beaver grey threads blended together and then three rows with the ecru thread. Repeat the previous six rows and then work four rows with the light and medium old gold threads blended together. Continue working rows of ghiordes knots with the black thread for the head. Trim the loops to approximately 6mm (¹/₄") and comb until fluffy. Trim the head slightly shorter than the body.

Legs and eyes

Embroider the legs with back stitch and attach two beads to the end of the head for eyes.

Applying the detached wings

Using the chenille needle, sink the wires of the wings at the sides of the body. Secure the wires on the back of the fabric and trim excess wire.

Finishing

Stamens

On the half of the rose centre not covered by the bee, work approximately nine pistil stitches of

EMBROIDERY KEY

All embroidery is worked with one strand of thread unless otherwise specified.

Stems and leaves

Stems = H and J
(whipped chain stitch)

Leaves

Outline = H (split back stitch)

Filling = H (satin stitch)

Centre vein = J (straight stitch)

Serrations = H
(single feather stitch)

Ladybird

Wings = C (padded satin stitch),
B (straight stitch)

Head = B (satin stitch)

Spots = B (French knot, 1 wrap)

Wild rose

Centre = I
(2 strands, ghiordes knot)

varying lengths over the petals. Using the same thread, add several ghiordes knots. Cut the loops to 8mm (⁵/₁₆") but do not comb them.

Shaping

Shape the rose petals by placing your finger behind each one and gently moulding the petal around it.

Detached petals

Outline = K
(couching, blanket stitch)

Filling = K, L and N
(long and short stitch)

Stamens = M
(pistil stitch, ghiordes knot)

Bee

Wings

Outline = F
(couching, overcast stitch)

Markings = O (fly stitch)

Body = A, B blended with G, and
D blended with E
(2 strands or 1 strand of each, ghiordes knot)

Head = B
(2 strands, ghiordes knot)

Legs = B (back stitch)

Eyes = P (beading)

by Anna Scott

- ELIZABETHAN BOUQUET -

THIS DESIGN USES

Back stitch, Beading, Blanket stitch, Buttonhole stitch, Chain stitch

Couching, Cretan stitch, Detached chain, Fern stitch, Fly stitch, French knot

Long and short stitch, Needleweaving, Overcast stitch, Padded satin stitch

Satin stitch, Split back stitch, Stem stitch, Straight stitch

Whipped stem stitch, Whipping, Wirework

MATERIALS

Threads, beads and needles

DMC stranded cotton

A = 730 very dark olive green
B = 742 light tangerine
C = 743 yellow
D = 744 light yellow
E = 758 very light terra cotta
F = 830 dark golden olive
G = 844 very dark beaver grey
H = 935 very dark avocado green
I = 936 dark avocado green
J = 3012 medium khaki green
K = 3051 dark green-grey
L = 3827 very light golden brown

Kreinik blending filament

M = 025 grey

Kreinik metallic cord

N = 005C black

Maria George size 11/0 seed bead

O = 6150 salmon

Mill Hill antique glass beads

P = 03042 indigo

No. 8 crewel needle
No. 10 crewel needle
No. 10 beading needle
No. 24 tapestry needle
Long darner

Supplies

Main fabric

Backing fabric

Pink homespun
15cm (6") square

Yellow homespun 15cm (6") square

Green homespun 15cm (6") square

Fusible webbing 20mm x 11mm
wide (3/4" x 1/2")

Mokuba no. 1500 silver organza
ribbon 20mm x 11mm wide
(3/4" x 1/2")

1.1m (1yd 7 1/4") no. 28 gauge
uncovered wire

Embroidery hoop
10cm (4") diameter

Embroidery hoop
15cm (6") diameter

ORDER OF WORK

Use the long darner when sinking the wires, the beading needle for attaching the beads and the tapestry needle for whipping and needle-weaving. The no. 10 crewel needle is used when stitching with one strand of thread and the no. 8 crewel needle when stitching with more than one strand.

Transfer the design using your chosen method and mount the main fabric in the larger hoop.

Stems

Rose stems

Stitch a row of stem stitch and then work a row of blanket stitch along each side. Whip all three rows together using blended threads and ensuring the threads remain untwisted.

Stitch a row of whipped stem stitch for the stem leading to the bud.

Carnation and lily stems

Embroider two parallel rows of stem stitch for one stem. Closely whip the two rows together. Work the second stem in the same manner.

Leaves on main fabric

Fern fronds

Beginning at the tip and working towards the base, stitch each frond with fern stitch.

Rose leaf

Outline the leaf with blanket stitch, ensuring the spokes of the stitches point outwards. Work the centre vein with chain stitch. Pad each half of the leaf with straight stitches that are parallel to the centre vein.

Cover the padding with satin stitch, enclosing the inner section of the blanket stitches *(diag 1)*.

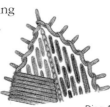

Diag 1

Narrow leaves

Outline the leaves with stem stitch and work a row of chain stitch on either side of the centre for padding. Working one side at a time, fill the leaves with satin stitch. Stitch rows of stem stitch close together to fill the curled tip of the leaf on the right.

Detached leaves

Place the green homespun in the smaller hoop and transfer the three leaf shapes.

Cut a 15cm (6") length of wire for the narrow leaf. Leaving a tail of wire at the base of the leaf, couch

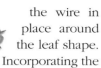

the wire in place around the leaf shape. Incorporating the couching stitches, embroider closely packed blanket stitches over the wire to completely cover it. Work a row of chain stitch on either side of the centre for padding. Fill the leaf with cretan stitch.

The two remaining leaves are worked in the same manner but different thread colours are used. Cut two lengths of wire, each 10cm (4") long. Couch a wire to the centre vein of one leaf. Work overcast stitch along the centre vein, covering the wire. Outline the leaf with split stitch. Cover the split stitch with closely worked blanket stitch, keeping the purls to the outside. Pad each half of the leaf with straight stitches parallel to the centre vein. Using a different thread colour for each half, cover the padding with satin stitch. Stitch the remaining leaf in the same manner.

Carefully cut out the leaves and set them aside.

Rose and rosebud

Embroidery on main fabric

Outline the rose petals with blanket stitches of varying lengths. Keep the stitches close together and the stitch direction towards the centre. Fill in the remainder of the petals with long and short stitch. Work two detached chains, one inside the other, for the sepal between each petal.

Stitch a stem stitch outline around the rosebud. Using the lighter shade of yellow at the tip and changing to the darker shade approximately halfway down, embroider the petals with long and short stitch. Beginning at the top of the stem, stitch five detached chains over the base of the bud for sepals.

Detached rose petals

Place the yellow homespun in the smaller hoop and transfer the petal shapes. Cut five pieces of wire, each 12cm (4 3/4") long.

Beginning and ending at the base of one petal and leaving two tails of wire, couch a length of wire in place around the petal shape.

Cover the wire with blanket stitch. Using the lightest shade of yellow at the top and the darker shade near the base, fill the petal with long and short stitch. Embroider the remaining petals in the same manner. Carefully cut out each petal and set them aside.

Carnation

Work long straight stitches from the base of the flower to the seven marked dots. Add a slightly shorter straight

stitch on either side of each long stitch (*diag 2*). Using a long length of thread, needleweave

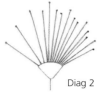

Diag 2

each group of three straight stitches together. Pull the thread firmly at the base and ease the tension as you work towards the top of the petal. When the ends of the shorter straight stitches are reached, wrap the thread around the middle straight stitch until reaching the top. Add a French knot to the top of each shorter straight stitch and a bead to the top of the longer straight stitches.

Outline the calyx with back stitch and then pad it with four vertical straight stitches. Embroider a detached chain over the lower end of each petal. Cover the calyx with satin stitch.

Lily

Embroidery on main fabric

Working from the outer edge towards the centre, fill the two back petals with rows of stem stitch. Outline the lower sections of the side petals with stem stitch and fill in with padded satin stitch.

Embroider a straight stitch for each stamen, twisting the thread before pulling the needle through. At the top of each straight stitch, work two detached chains.

Detached petals

Place the pink homespun in the smaller hoop and transfer the petal shapes. Cut a 15cm (6") length of wire.

Beginning and ending at the base of the centre petal and leaving two tails of wire, couch a length of wire in place around the shape. Cover the wire with blanket stitch. Work a row of chain stitch on either side of the centre for padding. Fill the petal with cretan stitch.

Outline the side petals with split back stitch. Cover the split back stitch with closely worked blanket stitches, keeping the purls to the outside. Work vertical straight stitches for padding and cover this with satin stitch.

Carefully cut out each petal and set them aside.

Fly

Trace the wings onto the fusible webbing and fuse it to the organza ribbon. Cut out the wings and fuse them to the main fabric. Work a fly stitch on each wing for markings. Embroider satin stitches across the middle of the wings to create the thorax. Outline the abdomen with back stitches and pad with straight stitches. Using blended threads, cover the abdomen with satin stitch. Add the legs with back stitch and the antennae with two straight stitches in a 'V' shape. Secure two beads below the antennae for eyes. Work a small stitch over the thread between the beads to keeps them in place.

Applying the detached petals and leaves

Rose

Using the long darner, sink the wires of the rose petals. Sink the right hand wire of one petal with the left hand wire of the adjacent petal so the petals overlap. Secure the wires on the back of the fabric and trim excess wire. Fill the centre of the rose with closely packed French knots.

Lily

Stitch the detached sections of the side petals to the upper edge of the side petals embroidered on the main fabric. Take the stitches just through the blanket stitch edge.

Sink the wires of the centre petal at the base of the flower. Secure the wires on the back of the fabric and trim excess wire.

Work five detached chains over the base of the petals to form a foundation for needleweaving. Taking the needle through the fabric on either side of the calyx and beginning at the lower edge, work needleweaving across the detached chains until you reach their tips.

Leaves

Sink the wires of all three leaves through the same hole in the fabric. On the wrong side, bend each wire behind its leaf and secure. Trim off excess wire and gently stroke the leaves to shape them.

EMBROIDERY KEY

All embroidery is worked with one strand of thread unless otherwise specified.

Rose

Petals on main fabric = C (blanket stitch), B and C (long and short stitch)

Sepals = J and L (detached chain)

Detached petals

Outlines = D (couching, blanket stitch)

Filling = C and D (long and short stitch)

Stem = I (2 strands, stem stitch), H (blanket stitch), H blended with I (1 strand of each, whipping)

Centre = B blended with D (1 strand of each, French knot, 1 wrap)

Rosebud

Petals

Outline = C (stem stitch)

Filling = B and C (long and short stitch)

Sepals = K (2 strands, detached chain)

Stem = H blended with I (1 strand of each, whipped stem stitch)

Carnation

Petals

Petals = E (2 strands, straight stitch, needlewoven bar, whipping)

Tips of petals = E (2 strands, French knot, 1 wrap), O (beading)

Base of petals = J (detached chain)

Calyx

Outline = K (back stitch)

Padding = K (6 strands, straight stitch)

Filling = K (padded satin stitch)

Lily

Petals on main fabric

Back petals = E (stem stitch)

Outlines of side petals = L (stem stitch)

Padding for side petals = L (straight stitch)

Filling for side petals = L (padded satin stitch)

Detached petals

Outline of centre petal = L (couching, blanket stitch)

Padding for centre petal = L (2 strands, chain stitch)

Filling for centre petal = L (2 strands, cretan stitch)

Outlines of side petals = E (split back stitch, blanket stitch)

Padding for side petals = E (straight stitch)

Filling for side petals = E (padded satin stitch)

Stamens = B (2 strands, straight stitch: 1 strand, detached chain)

Calyx = J blended with K

(1 strand of each, detached chain, needleweaving)

Leaves on main fabric

Fern fronds = A (2 strands, fern stitch)

Rose leaf

Outline = H (blanket stitch)

Padding = H and K (2 strands, straight stitch)

Filling = H and K (padded satin stitch)

Centre vein = F (chain stitch)

Narrow leaves

Outlines = J (stem stitch)

Padding = J (chain stitch)

Filling = J (padded satin stitch)

Leaf curl on right hand leaf = J (stem stitch)

Detached leaves

Upper leaf

Outline = K (split back stitch, blanket stitch)

Padding = H and K (straight stitch)

Filling = H and K (padded satin stitch)

Centre vein = J (couching, overcast stitch)

Lower leaf

Outline = A (split back stitch, blanket stitch)

Padding = A and K (straight stitch)

Filling = A and K (padded satin stitch)

Centre vein = F (couching, overcast stitch)

Narrow leaf

Outlines = J (couching, blanket stitch)

Padding = J (chain stitch)

Filling = J (cretan stitch)

Fly

Wing markings = M (fly stitch)

Thorax = G (satin stitch)

Abdomen

Outline = G (back stitch)

Padding = G (2 strands, straight stitch)

Filling = G blended with M (1 strand of each, padded satin stitch)

Legs = N (back stitch)

Antennae = N (straight stitch)

Eyes = P (beading)

Spring Garland, *Inspirations* issue 38

- COTTONTAIL -

Beige felt
10cm x 15cm wide (4" x 6")

Fusible webbing
10cm x 15cm wide (4" x 6")

15cm (6") no. 28 gauge
uncovered wire

Embroidery hoop
10cm (4") diameter

Embroidery hoop
15cm (6") diameter

THIS DESIGN USES

Couching, Detached chain
Fly stitch, French knot
Ghiordes knot, Long and short stitch
Padded satin stitch, Overcast stitch
Satin stitch, Split back stitch
Stab stitch, Straight stitch
Wirework

ORDER OF WORK

Use the chenille needle for sinking the wires, the no. 6 crewel needle when stitching with the chenille à broder and the no. 9 crewel needle for all other embroidery.

Transfer the design using your chosen method and mount the main fabric in the larger hoop.

Rabbit

Transfer the padding shapes for the body to the fusible webbing. Fuse

MATERIALS

Threads, charms and needles

Anchor stranded cotton
A = 2 white
B = 92 light bright purple
C = 95 light lilac
D = 144 light sky blue
E = 264 very light avocado green
F = 265 light avocado green
G = 266 avocado green
H = 281 dark olive
I = 301 butter yellow
J = 303 pumpkin
K = 372 very light hazelnut brown
L = 373 light hazelnut brown
M = 374 hazelnut brown
N = 375 dark hazelnut brown
O = 403 black

P = 1020 very light salmon
Q = 1050 coffee brown

Anchor Marlitt stranded rayon
R = 800 white
S = 895 very light pine green

Au Ver à Soie, chenille à broder
T = 3333 purple grape

Mill Hill glass treasures
U = 12126 butterflies (2)

No. 6 crewel needle
No. 9 crewel needle
No. 22 chenille needle

Supplies

Main fabric

Backing fabric

Quilter's muslin
15cm (6") square

to the felt and cut out. Centre the smaller piece of body padding within the outline on the main fabric and attach with stab stitches. Centre the larger piece over the first and attach in the same manner.

Head, body and ear on main fabric

Outline the head, body and ear with split back stitch. Using the photograph as a guide to colour placement, fill in with long and short stitch. Embroider the ear in the same manner.

Eye and tail

Stitch the eye with padded satin stitch and outline it with a fly stitch at each end. Add a white satin stitch spot to the eye.

Fill the tail with closely packed ghiordes knots. Trim the loops and comb until fluffy. Cut the pile shorter on the edges than in the centre.

Detached ear

Transfer the ear design to the quilter's muslin and mount it in the smaller hoop. Apply the padding in the same manner as the body padding.

Leaving two tails of wire, shape and couch the wire to the outline. Cover the wire with overcast stitch. Fill the outer ear and then the inner ear with long and short stitch. Carefully cut out the ear and set it aside.

Garden

Stitch a yellow French knot for the centre of each forget-me-not and surround these with five blue French knots for the petals.

Embroider five evenly spaced detached chains for the petals of the pink daisies. Work straight stitches between them. Add single French knots for the centres. Stitch long straight stitches for the stems and add detached chain leaves.

Embroider a very loose French knot for each carnation and work the stems with straight stitch. Scatter pink and white French knots among the other flowers for small buds.

Work the grass with ghiordes knots, intermingling the thread colours.

Butterflies

Paint the butterflies with clear nail polish and allow to dry. Work two stitches between the body and wings to secure them to the fabric.

Applying the detached ear

Sink the wires and secure on the back. Trim off excess wire. Gently stroke the ear to shape it.

EMBROIDERY KEY

All embroidery is worked with one strand of thread unless otherwise specified.

Rabbit

Head, body and ear on main fabric

Outlines = L (split back stitch)

Filling = K, L, M, N and Q
(long and short stitch)

Detached ear

Outline = N
(couching, overcast stitch)

Outer ear = K, L, M, N and Q
(long and short stitch)

Inner ear = P (long and short stitch)

Eye = O (padded satin stitch,
fly stitch), A (satin stitch)

Tail = A (2 strands, ghiordes knot)

Garden

Forget-me-nots

Centre = I
(3 strands, French knot, 1 wrap)

Petals = D
(3 strands, French knot, 1 wrap)

Pink daisies

Centre = J
(2 strands, French knot, 1 wrap)

Petals = B
(detached chain, straight stitch)

Stems = H (straight stitch)

Leaves = H (detached chain)

Carnations

Flower = T
(French knot, 1 wrap)

Stems = S (straight stitch)

Small buds = C and R
(3 strands, French knot, 1 wrap)

Grass = E, F and G
(3 strands, ghiordes knot)

Butterflies = P and U (couching)

by Jan Kerton

- BERRY GARLAND -

THIS DESIGN USES

Beading, Blanket stitch, Double running stitch, Drizzle stitch

French knot, Needlewoven picot, Running stitch, Stab stitch, Stem stitch

Straight stitch, Tufting, Whipping, Wrapping

MATERIALS

Threads, beads and needles

DMC stranded cotton
A = 115 variegated ruby
B = 310 black
C = 823 navy blue
D = 3828 hazelnut brown

Au Ver à Soie, Soie d'Alger
E = 2131 very light olive green
F = 2132 light olive green
G = 2134 medium olive green
H = 2924 light raspberry

Gumnut Yarns 'Stars' stranded silk
I = 859 ultra dark salmon pink

Madeira stranded metallic thread
J = 5014 black-gold

Mill Hill glass seed beads
K = 02014 black
L = 03024 mocha

Mill Hill frosted glass beads
M = 60367 frosted garnet
N = 62014 frosted black

No. 7 straw (milliner's) needle
No. 8 crewel needle
No. 9 crewel needle
No. 26 tapestry needle

Supplies

Main fabric

Backing fabric

Black felt
5cm x 8cm wide (2" x 3 1/8")

Red felt
5cm x 8cm wide
(2" x 3 1/8")

White felt
5cm x 8cm wide
(2" x 3 1/8")

Water-soluble fabric
10cm x 100cm wide
(4" x 39 1/2")

Polyester fibre-fill

12 round beads
8mm (5/16") diameter

26 pebble beads

Embroidery hoop
18cm (7") diameter

ORDER OF WORK

Use the no. 26 tapestry needle for needleweaving, wrapping and whipping, the straw needle for working drizzle stitch and the no. 8 crewel needle when working with the metallic thread. The no. 9 crewel needle is used for attaching the beads and for all other embroidery.

Transfer the design using your chosen method and mount the main fabric in the hoop.

Cut the water-soluble fabric into ten 10cm (4") squares.

Stems, leaves and tendrils

Embroider the stems and tendrils with double running stitch. Beginning at the tip of each stem or tendril, whip each running stitch.

Starting at the base, outline each half of one leaf and then stitch the centre vein with double running stitch. Whip the vein but not the outlines. Covering the outline and beginning both halves at the base, fill the leaf with blanket stitch. Embroider all remaining leaves in the same manner.

Strawberries

Ripe strawberries

Transfer and cut out three ripe strawberry shapes from the red felt. Fold one piece of felt in half so the straight sides meet. Whip the two straight edges together. Turn the felt through to the other side, carefully pushing out the point of the berry.

Work small running stitches around the upper edge. Fill the berry with fibre-fill and pull up the running stitches to gather the top. Tie off the threads securely.

Using silk thread, take the needle through the berry from top to bottom. Work three long stem stitches from the base to the top. Repeat this procedure until the felt is completely covered or 'coloured in'. As the tip fills, bring the thread out further up the berry. Embroider small straight stitches over the previous stitching with metallic thread to represent seeds.

Wrap the berry in water-soluble fabric and tie at the base to form a little handle *(diag 1)*. Mark the centre top. Beginning at the centre mark, work four needle-woven picots for the sepals.

Diag 1

Work the remaining two ripe strawberries in the same manner and set the strawberries aside.

Unripe strawberries

Transfer and cut out two larger and two smaller unripe strawberry shapes from the white felt. Using different thread colours, work the four berries in the same manner as the ripe strawberries. If desired, anchor the sepals to the berries with matching thread. Set the strawberries aside.

Red currants

Small currants

Using a 1m (39 ½") length of thread and leaving a 15cm (6") tail, wrap a pebble bead. Roll the bead between your fingers to ensure the wraps are evenly distributed.

Once the pebble bead is completely covered, thread a seed bead onto the needle. Take the needle back through the pebble bead and tie the two threads together. Trim the tails to 15cm (6"). The tails will be used to secure the currant to the fabric.

Repeat to make five more small currants and set them aside.

Large currants

Wrap a large round bead in the same manner as the small currants. Once the bead is completely covered, take the needle through the bead to the top. Attach 3 - 5 seed beads to the top. Take the thread to the base of the bead and tie the tails of thread together. Trim the tails to

15cm (6"). The tails will be used to secure the currant to the fabric. Repeat to make five more large currants and set them aside.

Blackberries

Large blackberries

Transfer and cut out three blackberry shapes from the black felt. Fold one piece of felt in half so the straight sides meet. Whip the two straight edges and small curved edges together. Turn the felt through to the other side. Work small running stitches around the upper edge. Fill with fibre-fill and pull up the running stitches to gather. Tie off the threads securely.

Randomly stitch beads to the felt until it is completely covered. Add 3 - 5 drizzle stitch sepals to the top of the berry.

Make two more blackberries in the same manner and set them aside.

Medium blackberries

Using a 1m (39 ½") length of thread and leaving a 15cm (6") tail, wrap a pebble bead in the same manner as the small currants. When the hole is almost filled, take the needle back through the hole to the base of the bead, catching some of the threads as you do so. Tie the tails of thread together firmly and do not cut off.

Completely cover the wrapped bead with small beads, stitching them to the wrapped threads. Add 3 - 4 drizzle stitch sepals to the top of the berry.

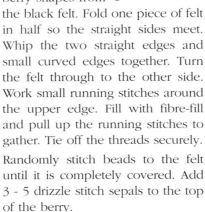

Make two more blackberries in the same manner and set them aside.

Small blackberries

Make two small blackberries using the following procedure.

Anchor a seed bead to the thread approximately 15cm (6") from the end. Add 6 - 8 beads, one at a time, stitching through the previous beads until a small uneven cluster forms. Stitch through the beads several times to ensure they are firmly held together. Tie the tails of thread together and trim to 15cm (6"). Set the blackberries aside.

Blueberries

Large blueberries

Using a 1m (39 ½") length of thread and leaving a 15cm (6") tail, wrap a large round bead in the same manner as the currants. When the hole is almost filled, take the needle back through the hole to the base of the bead, catching some of the threads as you do so. Roll the bead between your fingers to distribute the wraps evenly. Tie the tails of thread together firmly and do not cut off.

Anchor a new thread to the base of the berry. Take it through the hole to the top of the bead and work a small circle of blanket stitch around the hole. When the circle is complete, take the thread back through the hole to the base and anchor it. Do not cut off the thread.

Take the tails of thread through the hole to the top of the bead. Trim the threads to approximately 4mm (3/16") and comb until fluffy.

Make five more large blueberries in the same manner and set them aside.

Small blueberry

Using a pebble bead, make a small blueberry following the procedure for the large blueberries. Trim the tufts slightly shorter than the tufts on the large blueberries.

Cranberries

Wrap a pebble bead with thread in the same manner as the small currants. Take the thread to the base of the bead and tie the two tails of thread together. Knot a new thread and take it through the hole of the bead from the base to the top. Work a French knot over the hole and then take the thread back through the hole to the base.

Work fifteen more cranberries in the same manner.

Attaching the berries

Secure the strawberries to the main fabric first. For each one, use matching thread and work several stab stitches through the fabric and middle of the berry. Ensure the stitches lie in the same direction as the stem stitches and do not pull the stitches so tight that they distort the shape.

Attach the large blackberries to the fabric in the same manner as the strawberries.

Secure all other berries to the fabric with the tails of thread dangling from each one. To adjust the angle of a berry, use matching thread and take 1 - 2 stitches through the wrapping or beads on the side.

Strawberry Fields, *Inspirations* issue 42

EMBROIDERY KEY

All embroidery is worked with one strand of thread unless otherwise specified.

Stems, leaves and tendrils

Stems = G (double running stitch, whipping)

Tendrils = G (double running stitch, whipping)

Leaves

Outline = G (double running stitch)

Centre vein = G (double running stitch, whipping)

Filling = G (blanket stitch)

Strawberries

Ripe strawberries

Berry = H (stem stitch)

Seeds = J (straight stitch)

Sepals = F (needlewoven picot)

Unripe strawberries

Berry = E and F (stem stitch)

Seeds = G (straight stitch)

Sepals = G (needlewoven picot)

Red currants

Berry = A (wrapping)

Tip = A and L (beading)

Blackberries

Large blackberries

Berry = B, K, M and N (beading)

Sepals = G (drizzle stitch)

Medium blackberries

Berry = B (wrapping), B, K, M and N (beading)

Sepals = G (drizzle stitch)

Small blackberries = B, K, M and N (beading)

Blueberries

Large blueberries

Berry = C (2 strands, wrapping)

Tip = C (2 strands, blanket stitch, tufting)

Small blueberry

Berry = C (wrapping)

Tip = C (blanket stitch, tufting)

Cranberries

Berry = I (wrapping)

Tip = D (French knot, 2 wraps)

by Anna Scott

- FISHWATCH -

MATERIALS

Threads and needles

Au Ver à Soie, Soie d'Alger

A = 641 very light burnt orange
B = 1042 light fuchsia
C = 1443 sky blue
D = 1715 dark Williamsburg blue
E = 2635 dark copper
F = 3024 medium pink plum

G = 3424 medium silver green
H = 3436 very dark tan
I = 5023 sea green
J = F9 dark camel

No. 9 crewel needle

No. 24 tapestry needle

Supplies

Main fabric
Backing fabric
Cotton wool
2 wobbly stick-on eyes
5mm (3/16") diameter
White machine sewing thread
Embroidery hoop 15cm (6")
diameter

ORDER OF WORK

Use the tapestry needle for working the raised chain stitch, raised stem stitch and corded detached blanket stitch. The crewel needle is used for all other embroidery.

Mount the main fabric in the hoop and transfer the design using your chosen method.

Octopus

The head, tentacles and rock are padded with cotton wool, packed firmly and held in place with machine sewing thread. You will need more cotton wool that you might think. Apply it gradually until the desired effect is achieved.

Body

Roll cotton wool into a ball until it is quite firm. Shape the ball to fit the body of the octopus. Position the ball on the fabric and stitch in place with long stitches from side to side, keeping the stitches just inside the outline *(diag 1)*.

Diag 1

Continue adding extra cotton wool and stitching it in place until the body is very raised and rounded. Keep the body more raised at the upper end and allow it to slope towards the tentacles.

Using the plum thread, work parallel straight stitches, spaced 2mm (1/16") apart, across the body. Stitch a row of raised stem stitch along the centre. Working from the centre outwards each time, cover both halves with raised stem stitch.

Tentacles

For each tentacle, roll a piece of cotton wool into a sausage, tapering to a point at one end. Shape and pad each tentacle in a similar manner to the head.

Cover each tentacle with corded detached blanket stitch, beginning at the top and working towards the tip.

Eyes

After all embroidery is complete, remove the paper from the back of each eye and stick in place.

Rock

Pad the rock in the same manner as the body. This padding should sit higher than the tentacle resting on it.

Work a foundation of vertical straight stitches, spaced 1.5mm (1/16") apart, over the rock.

Using the three thread colours randomly, cover the rock with horizontal rows of chain stitch, working each stitch around a foundation stitch. Scatter French knots over the rock.

Sand and water

Scatter seed stitches below the octopus for grains of sand.

For the water, embroider long horizontal straight stitches of random lengths. Couch each stitch in place using the same thread.

EMBROIDERY KEY

All embroidery is worked with two strands of thread unless otherwise specified.

Octopus

Body = F (raised stem stitch)

Tentacles = A, B, E and F (corded detached blanket stitch)

Rock = H, I and J (raised chain stitch), I and J (French knot, 1 wrap)

Sand = J (seed stitch)

Water = C, D and G (couching, straight stitch)

by Lizzie Kulinski

- HENRY -

THIS DESIGN USES

Blanket stitch, Detached blanket stitch, Fly stitch, Long and short stitch

Overcast stitch, Raised stem stitch, Satin stitch, Split back stitch, Stab stitch, Stem stitch

Straight stitch, Wrapping

MATERIALS

Threads and needles

Anchor stranded cotton
A = 302 light pumpkin

DMC stranded cotton
B = 309 deep rose
C = 310 black
D = 333 very dark blue-violet
E = 680 dark old gold

Gumnut Yarns 'Tulips' hand-dyed natural mohair
F = 748 very dark daffodil
G = 945 medium hazelnut

DMC Broder Médicis fine wool
H = 8514 medium flesh

No. 9 crewel needle
No. 22 chenille needle

Supplies

Main fabric

Backing fabric

Gold felt 15cm (6") square

Fusible webbing 15cm (6") square

3 round wooden beads
12mm (1/2") diameter

Embroidery hoop
10cm (4") diameter

Embroidery hoop
20cm (8") diameter

ORDER OF WORK

Use the crewel needle when stitching with the stranded cotton and the chenille needle for all other embroidery.

Mount the main fabric in the larger hoop and transfer the design using your chosen method.

Bear

Trace the shapes for the ears, head, arm and body onto the right side of the fusible webbing. Fuse to the felt.

Ears

Mount the felt in the smaller hoop. Cover the outer section of each ear with long and short stitch. Add a layer of straight stitches over this first layer. Fill the inner ears with satin stitch. Carefully cut out each ear and overcast the edges to ensure the felt is completely covered. Set the ears aside. They will be attached after the rest of the bear is complete. Cut out all remaining pieces.

Attaching the felt

Stitch along each design line in split back stitch. Position the smaller piece of felt for the face onto the right side of the fabric. Attach with several tiny stab stitches. Position the larger piece of felt over the first and attach in the same manner.

Repeat the procedure for the two pieces of felt for the tummy and the single piece for the right arm.

Head

Starting at the centre of the muzzle and stitching towards the outer edge, completely cover the felt with long and short stitch. Embroider little 'stray' stitches over the edge to represent fluffy fur.

Stitch the eyes and nose with horizontal satin stitches. Add a tiny straight stitch and two fly stitches for the mouth. Beginning and ending at the outer edges of the mouth, outline the muzzle with split back stitch.

Using the brown mohair, work several straight stitches under the chin to create a shadowed effect.

Body

Beginning at the neck and working away from the centre seamline of the tummy, work the body in the same manner as the head.

Arms and legs

Work the right arm in the same manner as the head and body, stitching the fur so it parts down the centre of the arm. Embroider the left arm and then the legs. Begin each leg at the hip and work towards the foot, keeping all the stitches in the same direction. Outline the body and inside of the right paw with split back stitch.

Stitch the paws of the left arm and legs with long and short stitch. Add the paw pads with satin stitch and the claws with straight stitch.

Attaching the ears

Push a pin through the base of one ear and pin it to the top of the head at the marked position. Keeping the ear upright and using tiny straight stitches, secure the base of the ear as close as possible to the head. Embroider several straight stitches over the base of the ear and top of the head to fill in any remaining spaces.

Attach the second ear in the same manner.

Beach ball

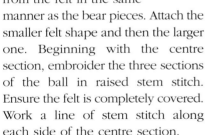

Transfer and cut out the shapes for the ball from the felt in the same manner as the bear pieces. Attach the smaller felt shape and then the larger one. Beginning with the centre section, embroider the three sections of the ball in raised stem stitch. Ensure the felt is completely covered. Work a line of stem stitch along each side of the centre section.

Shadows

Embroider the shadows below the bear and balls with long straight stitches.

Juggling balls

Leaving a 10cm (4") tail of thread, wrap one wooden bead with the pumpkin thread. Leave a 10cm (4") tail at the end for securing. Using a new thread, take it up through the centre of the bead and secure with a small stitch through the wrapping. Wrap the thread twice around the top of the bead to form a couronne. Cover the bead in detached blanket stitch, increasing and decreasing the number of stitches in each row to fit the shape of the bead. When reaching the base of the bead, secure the last stitch with two tiny back stitches. Do not cut off the excess thread.

Thread the tails of thread into the chenille needle and take them to the back of the fabric at the marked position. Secure the tails firmly on the back of the fabric.

Create and attach the blue-violet and rose balls in the same manner.

Papillon, *Inspirations* issue 26

EMBROIDERY KEY

All embroidery is worked with one strand of thread unless otherwise specified.

Bear

Outlines = F (split back stitch)

Outer ears = F
(long and short stitch,
straight stitch, overcast stitch)

Inner ears = H (satin stitch)

Head = F (long and short stitch,
straight stitch)

Shadow under chin = G
(straight stitch)

Eyes = C (satin stitch)

Nose = C (satin stitch)

Mouth = C (fly stitch)

Muzzle outline = E
(split back stitch)

Body, arms and legs = F (long
and short stitch, straight stitch)

Tummy and arm outline = G
(split back stitch)

Paws = H (long and short stitch)

Paw pads = C (satin stitch)

Claws = C (straight stitch)

Beach ball = A, B and D
(raised stem stitch),
B (stem stitch)

Juggling balls = A, B and D
(wrapping, blanket stitch,
detached blanket stitch)

Shadows = E (straight stitch)

by Janet Luce

- RAINBOW LORIKEET -

MATERIALS

Threads, beads and needles

DMC stranded cotton
A = 356 medium terra cotta
B = 471 very light avocado green
C = 472 ultra light avocado green
D = 523 light fern green
E = 610 very dark taupe
F = 702 Kelly green
G = 703 light Kelly green
H = 740 tangerine
I = 741 medium tangerine
J = 742 light tangerine
K = 743 yellow
L = 745 very light yellow
M = 791 very dark cornflower blue
N = 792 dark cornflower blue
O = 817 very dark coral red
P = 840 medium beige
Q = 841 light beige
R = 946 medium burnt orange
S = 3031 brown groundings

Mill Hill antique glass beads
T = 03049 rich red

Mill Hill frosted glass beads
U = 62036 pink coral

Mill Hill glass seed bead
V = 02014 black

No. 3 straw (milliner's) needle
No. 10 crewel needle
No. 10 beading needle
Long darner

THIS DESIGN USES

Beading, Blanket stitch, Bullion knot, Couching, Fly stitch
Long and short stitch, Overcast stitch, Satin stitch, Split back stitch
Stab stitch, Stem stitch, Straight stitch, Wirework

Supplies

Main fabric

Backing fabric

Quilter's muslin 15cm (6") square

Cream felt 10cm (4") square

Fusible webbing 10cm (4") square

40cm (16") no. 30 gauge green covered wire

Embroidery hoop 20cm (8") diameter

Embroidery hoop 10cm (4") diameter

ORDER OF WORK

Use the long darner when sinking wires, the beading needle for attaching the beads, the straw needle for working the bullion knots and the crewel needle for all other embroidery.

Transfer the design using your chosen method and mount the main fabric in the larger hoop.

Rainbow lorikeet

Padding

Transfer the padding shapes for the body and wings to the fusible webbing. Fuse to the felt and cut out each piece. Centre the smallest piece of body padding within the outline on the main fabric and attach with stab stitches. Centre the medium size piece over the first and attach in the same manner. Position the largest felt piece over the previous pieces and attach as before, keeping the stab stitches close together.

Attach the padding for the wings following the same procedure.

Head, body, wings and tail

Outline the head, body, wings and tail with split back stitch. Using the photograph as a guide to colour placement, fill in the head and body with long and short stitch. Embroider satin stitch stripes over the padded sections of the wings.

Fill in the tail and lower section of wing with long and short stitch. Add markings to the upper tail with blanket stitch and then embroider eight fly stitches on the lower tail for markings.

Beak and eye

Outline the beak with split back stitch and then fill in with long and short stitch. Working over the previous stitching, add a satin stitch spot for the eye. Attach a black bead in the centre of the spot.

Claws

Work the claws after the branch is embroidered. Stitch two bullion knots side by side for each claw.

Branch

Leaves on main fabric

Outline each leaf with split back stitch and then fill in each half with slanting satin stitches that cover the split back stitch. Embroider the centre veins and stems with split back stitch. Add straight stitches, which lie in the same direction as the satin stitches, for the leaf markings.

Detached leaves

Place the quilter's muslin in the smaller hoop and transfer the leaf shapes. Cut two lengths of wire, each 20cm (8") long.

Beginning at the tip of one leaf, couch a wire in place along the centre vein. Cover the wire with overcast stitch for the length of the vein. Shape the wire to fit the outline and couch in place *(diag 1)*. Embroider closely packed blanket stitches over the wire to completely cover it and then a row of split back stitch just inside the blanket stitch edging. Work slanting satin stitches in each half of the leaf enclosing the split back stitch outline. Add straight stitches that lie in the same direction as the satin stitches for the leaf markings. Repeat for the remaining leaf.

Carefully cut out the leaves and set them aside.

Diag 1

Branch

Using the photograph as a guide to colour placement, stitch the branch with rows of stem stitch worked closely together.

Blossoms

Within each blossom, use the two bead colours randomly. Secure a bead at the centre of one blossom and then secure a second bead directly below. Thread 5 - 9 beads onto the needle. Take the needle through the second secured bead and pull the beads into a rough circle. Take the needle through the beads again and then work small couching stitches between them. Fashion four more blossoms in the same manner.

At the end of the branch, secure six beads in a curved line.

Applying the detached leaves

Using the long darner, sink the wires and secure on the back of the fabric. Trim off excess wire. Gently stroke the leaves to shape them.

EMBROIDERY KEY

All embroidery is worked with one strand of thread unless otherwise specified.

Rainbow lorikeet

Outlines = E (split back stitch)

Head = B, C, F, G, M and N (long and short stitch)

Body = H, I, J, K, M, N and R (long and short stitch)

Tail = B, C, G, K and L (long and short stitch)

Upper tail markings = F (blanket stitch)

Lower tail markings = B (fly stitch)

Wings = F and G (long and short stitch, satin stitch)

Beak = I and O (long and short stitch)

Eye = O (satin stitch), V (beading)

Claws = S (bullion knot, 15 wraps)

Branch

Leaves on main fabric

Outlines = D (split back stitch)

Filling = D (satin stitch)

Centre vein = A (split back stitch)

Markings = A (straight stitch)

Stems = A (split back stitch)

Detached leaves

Outlines = D (couching, blanket stitch, split back stitch)

Filling = D (satin stitch)

Centre vein = A (couching, overcast stitch)

Markings = A (straight stitch)

Branch = P and Q (stem stitch)

Blossoms = T and U (beading)

Nature's Jewel, *Inspirations* issue 36

by Trish Burr

- OUT OF AFRICA -

MATERIALS

Threads, beads and needles

DMC stranded cotton
A = 310 black
B = 317 pewter grey
C = 318 light steel grey
D = 349 dark coral
E = 350 medium coral
F = 420 dark hazelnut brown
G = 433 medium brown
H = 434 light brown
I = 435 very light brown
J = 436 tan
K = 437 light tan
L = 543 ultra light beige
M = 580 dark moss green
N = 581 moss green
O = 701 light Christmas green
P = 702 Kelly green
Q = 703 light Kelly green
R = 704 very light Kelly green
S = 712 cream
T = 721 medium orange spice
U = 722 light orange spice
V = 726 golden yellow
W = 728 topaz
X = 734 light olive green
Y = 738 very light tan
Z = 761 light salmon
AA = 782 dark topaz
AB = 783 medium topaz
AC = 817 very dark coral red
AD = 834 very light golden olive
AE = 898 very dark coffee brown
AF = 905 dark parrot green
AG = 906 medium parrot green
AH = 907 light parrot green
AI = 958 medium mint
AJ = 976 medium golden brown
AK = 977 light golden brown

AL = 3046 medium yellow-beige
AM = 3687 tea rose
AN = 3688 medium tea rose
AO = 3705 dark melon
AP = 3706 medium melon
AQ = 3803 light wine
AR = 3819 chartreuse
AS = 3828 hazelnut brown
AT = 3846 light bright turquoise
AU = 3856 ultra light mahogany
AV = 3862 dark latté
AW = 3864 light latté

DMC soft tapestry cotton
AX = 2421 tan
AY = 2471 light yellow-green

DMC stranded metallic thread
AZ = 5279 copper

Kreinik blending filament
BB = 015 chartreuse
BC = 028 citron
BD = 032 pearl

Kreinik metallic cord
BE = 104C colonial gold
BF = 215C antique copper

Kreinik hi-lustre metallic braid
BG = 017HL white gold

Kreinik very fine metallic braid
BH = 021 copper
BI = 210 gold dust

Madeira no. 30 metallic thread
BJ = 6033 gold

Madeira no. 30 rayon thread
BK = 1126 tan
BL = 1270 light gold

Madeira no. 40 rayon thread
BM = 1071 pearl white

Mill Hill glass seed beads
BN = 02011 Victorian gold

Mill Hill antique glass beads
BO = 03025 wildberry

Mill Hill petite glass beads
BP = 42011 Victorian gold
BQ = 42030 Victorian copper

Mill Hill pebble beads
BR = 05025 ruby

No. 9 crewel needle
No. 10 crewel needle
No. 12 beading needle
No. 22 chenille needle
No. 24 chenille needle
No. 26 chenille needle

Supplies

Main fabric

Backing fabric

Medium weight interfacing
15cm x 75cm wide (6" x 29 1/2")

Fusible webbing
15cm x 45cm wide (6" x 18")

White organza
15cm x 30cm wide (6" x 12")

Cream organza
15cm x 30cm wide (6" x 12")

Lemon organza 15cm (6") square

Gold organza 15cm (6") square

Small amount of polyester fibre-fill

50cm (20") natural coloured raffia

1.3m (1yd 15") no. 28 gauge
uncovered wire

Embroidery hoop
25cm (10") diameter

Embroidery hoop
10cm (4") diameter

ORDER OF WORK

Use the no. 10 crewel needle when stitching with one strand of thread, the no. 9 crewel needle for two strands and the no. 24 chenille needle for four strands. The no. 26 chenille needle is used for the raffia and the no. 22 chenille needle for sinking wires and attaching twisted cord. Attach all beads with the beading needle.

Mount the main fabric in the larger hoop and transfer the design using your chosen method.

Carmine Bee Eater bird

Branch and leaves

Outline the branch with stem stitch and fill with closely packed French knots. Using stem stitch, embroider all the leaf stems and the centre veins of the two leaves on the main fabric. Fill each side of these leaves with padded satin stitch.

Bird

Outline the head, body, beak and wings with split stitch.

Trace the body and wing shapes onto the interfacing and cut out. The wing shape is slightly larger than the outline on the fabric to allow for padding.

Attach both shapes to the main fabric with stab stitch, leaving an opening at the top of the wing. Insert a small amount of fibre-fill into the wing and close the opening.

Stitch the tip of the far wing and the lower body with satin stitch. Embroider the beak, then throat, chest and padded wing with long and short stitch. Use the photograph as a guide to thread colour. Work rows of closely packed ghiordes knots across the head. Trim the loops very short and comb them until a velvety pile is achieved.

Outline the eye and beak with split stitch. Work the claws and legs with split stitch and then add 3 - 4 straight stitches to the lower body.

Attach a bead for the eye, securing it with two small stitches so the hole faces outwards.

Detached leaves

Transfer three leaf shapes to the interfacing and mount the fabric in the smaller hoop.

Embroider the outlines and centre veins with split stitch. Cut three pieces of wire, each 8cm (3 1/8") long. On the wrong side of the interfacing, shape one length of wire as shown *(diag 1)*. Couch in place. On the right side, pad each half of the leaf with satin stitches that run from the base to the tip. Stitching from the centre

Diag 1

vein, cover the outline and padding with closely worked blanket stitch. Work the remaining two leaves in the same manner.

Carefully cut out the leaves. Sink the tails of wire at the positions indicated on the pattern and secure them on the back of the fabric.

Rhodesian holly

Branches and stems

Outline the base of the main branch with stem stitch. Grading from the darkest shade at the bottom to the lightest shade at the top, fill the branch with French knots. Embroider the leaf stems with stem stitch, continuing along the leaf vein for the surface embroidered leaf. Add straight stitches to the end of the main branch and for the stub above the berries.

Leaves

Embroider the leaf on the main fabric and the detached leaf following the same procedure as those on the bee eater's branch.

Berries

Using a long strand of the darkest coral thread, wrap a pebble bead until it is completely covered. Change to two strands of chartreuse thread. Attach a small bead to the end of the pebble bead. Thread all four strands into the needle. Take them to the back of the fabric just below the stub and secure. Make four more berries in the same manner, using the darkest coral thread for one more berry, the medium shade for two berries and the lightest coral shade for one berry. Attach them as before, varying the lengths of the stalks. Loosely catch 2 - 3 threads at the back of each berry to the main fabric to keep them in position.

Warthog and fly

Warthog

Stitch along all design lines, except for the tusk, with split stitch. Pad the sections shown in the diagram with horizontal satin stitches *(diag 2)*. Fill the head, body and legs with long and short stitch.

Diag 2

Use the photo-graph as a guide to thread colour placement. Fill the horn with straight stitches that use the same hole in the fabric at the tip.

Stitch over all outlines, including the eye, with split stitch. Attach a bead for the eye, securing it so the hole faces outwards.

Randomly embroider straight stitches along the edges of the legs, mane, lower body and face to create a shaggy appearance.

Fly

Outline the wings with split stitch and then fill with padded satin stitch. Using metallic thread, outline the head and body in the same manner. Embroider the legs and antennae, and then fill the head and body with satin stitch.

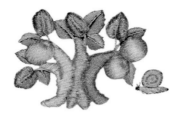

Baobab tree

Trunk and branches

Outline each section with split stitch. Couch lengths of soft cotton from the base of the trunk to the tips of the branches for padding. Work horizontal satin stitch over the padding, using the lightest shade on the left hand side and the darkest shade on the right hand side.

Stems and leaves

Embroider the leaf stems and veins of the surface embroidered leaves with stem stitch. Stitch the leaves on the main fabric in the same manner as those on the bee eater's branch.

Transfer four detached leaf shapes to the interfacing and mount in the smaller hoop. Stitch and attach the leaves in the same manner as the previous detached leaves.

Cream of tartar fruit

Transfer the fruit shapes to the inter-facing and mount in the smaller hoop. Outline each fruit with split stitch. Work horizontal satin stitches for padding and then cover this with vertical long and short stitches.

Leaving a 4mm (3/16") turning around all sides, cut out each fruit separately. Finger pressing the turning under as you go, attach one fruit to the main fabric with stab stitches. Leave a small opening at the top. Insert a small amount of fibre-fill, push the turning under and close the opening. Repeat for the two remaining fruit. To neaten the edges, add several straight stitches, which blend with the long and short stitches, to each fruit.

Near the top of each fruit, work 2 - 3 straight stitches side by side and pull firmly to form an indent.

Snail

Outline the body and work the feelers with split stitch. Fill the body with padded satin stitch.

Beginning from the centre, couch soft cotton in a spiral to pad the shell. Again, beginning from the centre, cover the padding with satin stitch. Attach a bead for the head.

Dung beetle and bee

Dung beetle

Outline the head and body with split stitch and pad each section with horizontal satin stitches. Cover the head and upper body with vertical satin stitches and the lower body with long and short stitch.

Embroider the legs with back stitch and add straight stitches to thicken those sections nearest the body.

Dung ball

Transfer the ball shape onto the interfacing and mount the fabric in the smaller hoop. Cover the entire shape with French knots and then randomly attach beads among the knots.

Leaving a 4mm (3/16") turning around all sides, cut out the ball. Finger pressing the turning under as you go, attach the ball to the main fabric with stab stitch. Leave a small opening at the top. Insert a small amount of fibre-fill, push the turning under and close the opening. Embroider a few French knots around the edge to cover the stab stitches.

Split the raffia into strands by making a small cut at one end and tearing downwards. Using one strand, work straight stitches at differing angles around the ball to depict dried grass. Add 3 - 4 loose straight stitches among the French knots.

Bee

Outline the body and thorax with split stitch and fill each body stripe with rows of closely packed ghiordes knots. Using metallic thread, add 2 - 3 ghiordes knots to each stripe, scattering them among the previous knots. Trim the loops and comb until fluffy. Cut the pile shorter

on the edges than in the centre to create a domed effect.

Work the legs with back stitch and the antennae with straight stitch.

Cut the white organza into two pieces, each 15cm (6") square. Mount the two pieces together in the smaller hoop and transfer the wing designs. Cut two pieces of wire, each 10cm (4") long. Shape one length of wire to fit one wing outline and couch in place. Overcast the wire to the fabric. Add two straight stitches for the wing markings. Repeat for the second wing.

Carefully cut out the wings as close as possible to the overcasting. Sink the wires at the marked positions and secure on the back of the fabric. Fill the thorax with satin stitch and attach two beads for eyes.

Giraffe

Outline the giraffe and his spots with split stitch. Work horizontal satin stitches across the head, body and legs, omitting the spots. Beginning with the lighter shade at the head and grading to the

darker shade on the rump, fill the head, body and closest legs with long and short stitch. Embroider the farthest two legs and ear separately.

Fill the spots with padded satin stitch without covering the outline. Add the tail, mouth and eye. Attach a bead for the eye, securing it so the hole faces outwards.

Stitch closely packed ghiordes knots for the mane. Trim the loops to approximately 3mm (1/8") and comb until fluffy.

Water berries and mopane worm

Branch

Stitch a row of stem stitch along the underside of the branch. Using the darkest shade near the lower edge and grading to the lightest near the top, fill the branch with French knots. Leave a small gap for the leaf and berry stems. Finish the ends with several straight stitches.

Leaves and stems

Work the leaf stems with adjacent rows of stem stitch. Continue the stem stitch along the leaf veins of the leaves on the main fabric. Work the four surface embroidered leaves and the two detached leaves in the same manner as those on the bee eater's branch.

Water berries

Transfer the berry shapes to the interfacing and create them in the same manner as the cream of tartar fruit, omitting the indent.

Using two strands of thread approximately 50cm (20") long, make a twisted cord. Work long loose straight stitches from the branch to the ends of the berries with the cord. Add a fourth straight stitch to the upper right leaf as well.

Mopane worm

Outline the body with split stitch and fill the head and tail with satin stitch. Embroider straight stitches for the stripes and spikes. Fill the sections between the stripes with ghiordes knots, alternating the thread colour from section to section. Trim the loops to approximately 3mm (1/8") and comb until fluffy.

Gypsy moth

Lower wings

Transfer the wing shapes to the lemon organza. Cut the cream organza into two 15cm (6") squares. Fuse one square to the back of the lemon organza with a piece of fusible webbing. Fuse a second layer of webbing to the back of the cream organza. Cut out the wings and position them on the main fabric. Fuse in place.

Outline each wing with two rows of stem stitch and then work the wing markings with straight stitches.

Upper wings

Transfer the wing shapes to the gold organza. Fuse the remaining square of cream organza to the back of the gold organza with a piece of fusible webbing. Mount the fabric in the smaller hoop. Cut two 15cm (6") lengths of wire.

Shape one length of wire to fit one wing outline and couch in place. Work closely packed blanket stitches over the wire, leaving the tails free. Use the brown thread for the side and upper section of the wing and the gold thread for the lower section.

Embroider the spot with satin stitch and then add straight stitches for the wing markings.

Repeat for the second wing.

Carefully cut out the wings as close as possible to the stitching. Sink the wires at the marked positions and secure on the back of the fabric. Bend the wings into shape.

Body

Outline the abdomen and thorax with split stitch and work the antennae with straight stitch. Fill the abdomen with closely worked ghiordes knots. Change thread colour and repeat for the thorax. Trim the loops to approximately 2mm (1/16") and comb until fluffy. Secure two beads to the base of the antennae for eyes.

THIS DESIGN USES

Back stitch, Beading

Blanket stitch, Couching

French knot, Ghiordes knot

Long and short stitch

Overcast stitch

Padded satin stitch, Satin stitch

Split stitch, Stem stitch

Straight stitch, Twisted cord,

Wirework, Wrapping

EMBROIDERY KEY

All embroidery is worked with one strand of thread unless otherwise specified.

Carmine Bee Eater bird

Bird

Head = AI (split stitch), AI blended with AT (1 strand of each, ghiordes knot)

Beak = B (split stitch), A and B (long and short stitch)

Throat and chest = AP (split stitch), Z, AO and AP (long and short stitch)

Lower body = AT (split stitch, satin stitch)

Lower body markings = A (straight stitch)

Wing = U (split stitch), T, U and AU (long and short stitch)

Tip of far wing = C (satin stitch)

Legs and claws = A (split stitch)

Eye = A (split stitch), BN (beading)

Branch

Outline = AV (stem stitch)

Filling = L, AV and AW (French knot, 2 wraps)

Stems = AD (stem stitch)

Leaves on fabric

Outlines = AF (split stitch)

Veins = AD (stem stitch)

Filling for leaf on left = AG and AH (padded satin stitch)

Filling for leaf on right = AF and AG (padded satin stitch)

Detached leaves

Outlines = AG (split stitch)

Veins = AD (stem stitch)

Attaching wire = AG (couching)

Filling = AG and AH (satin stitch, blanket stitch)

Rhodesian holly

Branches and stems

Main branch = I (stem stitch), I, J and Y (French knot, 2 wraps)

End of main branch = I and Y (straight stitch)

Leaf stems = J and K (stem stitch)

Stub = I and K (straight stitch)

Leaves

Outlines = AR (split stitch)

Vein of surface embroidered leaf = K (stem stitch)

Filling of surface embroidered leaf = N and AR (padded satin stitch)

Vein of detached leaf = K (stem stitch)

Attaching wire = AR (couching)

Filling of detached leaf = M and AR (satin stitch, blanket stitch)

Berries

Berries = D, E and AC (wrapping), BR (bead)

Tips = BO (beading)

Stalks = AR (4 strands)

Warthog and fly

Warthog

Outlines = J (split stitch)

Padding = J (satin stitch)

Head, body, legs, ears and tail = J, S and Y (long and short stitch)

Mane = S (long and short stitch)

Horn = S (straight stitch)

Details = A (split stitch)

Eye = A (split stitch), BP (beading)

Shaggy hairs = J, S and Y (straight stitch)

Fly

Wings = BM (split stitch, padded satin stitch)

Head and body = BH (split stitch, satin stitch)

Legs = BH (back stitch)

Antennae = BH (straight stitch)

Baobab tree

Trunk and branches

Outlines = F (split stitch)

Filling = AX (laid stitches), AS (couching), F, AL and AS (satin stitch)

Stems = X (stem stitch)

Leaves on fabric

Outlines = P (split stitch)

Veins = X (stem stitch)

Filling = P and R, or O and Q (padded satin stitch)

Detached leaves

Outlines = P (split stitch)

Veins = X (stem stitch)

Attaching wire = P (couching)

Filling = P and R (satin stitch), P blended with BB, and R blended with BC (1 strand of each, blanket stitch)

Cream of tartar fruit

Outlines = AA (split stitch)

Fruit = AA (satin stitch), V, W and AA (long and short stitch, straight stitch)

Indent = F (straight stitch)

Snail

Body = BE
(split stitch, padded satin stitch)

Feelers = BE (split stitch)

Shell = AY (laid thread),
AR (couching, satin stitch)

Head = BP (beading)

Dung beetle and bee

Dung beetle

Head and body outlines = H
(split stitch)

Head = H (padded satin stitch)

Upper body = K
(padded satin stitch)

Lower body = J and K (satin stitch,
long and short stitch)

Legs = BF
(back stitch, straight stitch)

Dung ball

Ball = H (2 strands, French knot,
2 wraps), BQ (beading)

Dried grass = raffia (straight stitch)

Bee

Body and thorax outlines = G
(split stitch)

Body = G and AB (2 strands,
ghiordes knot), AZ (ghiordes knot)

Thorax = G (satin stitch)

Legs = BE (2 strands, back stitch)

Antennae = BE
(2 strands, straight stitch)

Wings = BL (couching,
overcast stitch, straight stitch)

Eyes = BP (beading)

Giraffe

Body outlines = G (split stitch)

Filling for head, body and closest
legs = AK (satin stitch), AJ and AK
(long and short stitch)

Farthest front leg = AJ
(long and short stitch)

Farthest rear leg = H
(long and short stitch)

Farthest ear = H (straight stitch)

Spot outlines = S (split stitch)

Spot filling = AE
(padded satin stitch)

Tail = H (split stitch)

Mouth = A (straight stitch)

Eye = A (straight stitch),
BQ (beading)

Mane = AJ (2 strands, ghiordes knot)

Waterberries and mopane worm

Branch

Underside = I (stem stitch)

Filling = I, J and Y
(French knot, 2 wraps)

Ends = I and Y (straight stitch)

Stems = I and AD (stem stitch)

Leaves on fabric

Outlines = AF (split stitch)

Veins = AD (stem stitch)

Filling = AF and AH, or AG and
AR (padded satin stitch)

Detached leaves

Outlines = AF (split stitch)

Veins = AD (stem stitch)

Attaching wire = AF (couching)

Filling = AF and AH, or AG and
AR (satin stitch, blanket stitch)

Water berries

Outlines = AQ
(2 strands, split stitch)

Berries = AM (satin stitch), AM,
AN and AQ (long and short stitch,
straight stitch)

Stems = AD (2 strands, twisted
cord, straight stitch)

Mopane worm

Outline = BH (split stitch)

Head and tail = BH (satin stitch)

Stripes and spikes = BH
(straight stitch)

Body segments = AJ and AR
(2 strands, ghiordes knot)

Gypsy moth

Lower wings

Outlines = BI (stem stitch)

Markings = BD (straight stitch)

Upper wings

Outlines = BK and BL
(couching, blanket stitch)

Outer markings = BK
(straight stitch)

Spots = S (satin stitch)

Markings = BD (straight stitch)

Body

Abdomen outline = AV (split stitch)

Abdomen = AV
(2 strands, ghiordes knot)

Thorax outline = S (split stitch)

Thorax = S
(2 strands, ghiordes knot)

Antennae = BG (straight stitch)

Eyes = BP (beading)

by *Judy Stephenson*

- WILD PASSIONFRUIT -

PASSIFLORA FOETIDA

MATERIALS

Threads and needles

DMC stranded cotton

A = blanc
B = ecru
C = 730 very dark olive green
D = 732 olive green (2 skeins)
E = 733 medium olive green
F = 3835 medium grape

No. 5 straw (milliner's) needle

No. 22 tapestry needle

Long darner

Supplies

Main fabric

Backing fabric

Green poplin 15cm (6") square

Medium weight interfacing
15cm (6") square

Water-soluble fabric
15cm (6") square

61cm (24") no. 30 gauge green
covered wire

1.2m (1yd 11 ½") no. 30 gauge
white covered wire

Round wooden bead
8mm (⁵/₁₆") diameter

7 cream florist stamens

Embroidery hoop
20cm (8") diameter

Embroidery hoop
10cm (4") diameter

2 marbles

THIS DESIGN USES

Blanket stitch, Chain stitch

Couching, Detached blanket stitch

Ghiordes knot, Satin stitch

Stem stitch, Straight stitch

Whipped chain stitch

Wirework, Wrapping

ORDER OF WORK

Use the tapestry needle for working the detached blanket stitch, the long darner for separating threads and sinking wires, and the straw needle for all other embroidery.

Mount the main fabric in the larger hoop and transfer the design using your chosen method.

Stems and surface embroidered leaves

Stitch the main stem and the three leaf stems for the surface embroidered leaves with whipped chain stitch.

Outline each leaf with chain stitch and fill in with detached blanket stitch. Add straight stitches for the leaf veins.

Detached leaves

Transfer the two leaf shapes to the green poplin and mount the fabric in the smaller hoop. Stitch the leaves in the same manner as the surface embroidered leaves.

Cut two lengths of wire, each 20cm (8") long. Leaving a tail of wire extending at the beginning and end, couch green wire around each leaf. Covering the wire, outline the leaves with blanket stitches approximately 2mm (1/16") long. Cut out the leaves from the poplin, taking care not to cut any embroidery threads.

Secure a new thread at the base of the leaf. Wrap the thread around the tails of wire and secure but do not cut off the excess. Sink the tails of wire at the positions indicated on the pattern. Take the thread to the back of the fabric at the same position and secure the ends of the wrapped wire.

Flower

Transfer twelve petal shapes to the interfacing and mount it in the smaller hoop. Cut twelve pieces of white covered wire, each 10cm (4") long. Leaving a tail of wire extending at the beginning and end, couch a wire around one petal shape. Using the ecru thread, work blanket stitch around the petal in the same manner as the leaves. Fill each half of the petal with satin stitch and then work the centre vein with stem stitch. Create

five more ecru petals and then six white petals in the same manner. Carefully cut out all the petals.

On the main fabric, evenly space the ecru petals around the outside of the flower's marked centre circle. Sink the wires, bend them back underneath the petals and secure. Position the white petals just inside the circle of ecru petals, placing them so they lie between the ecru ones. Sink the wires, bend them back underneath the petals and secure.

Using the blanc thread, stitch two rows of ghiordes knots in a circle just inside the white petals. Change to the grape thread and stitch two more rows in the same manner. Cut the white loops to approximately 2cm (3/4") and the grape loops to approximately 1cm (3/8"). Brush the threads away from the centre and trim again if required.

Trim the stamens to 4cm (1 1/2") and hold them together in a bundle. Beginning 1cm (3/8") from the tips, wrap the wires for approximately 1cm (3/8"). Sink the ends through one hole at the centre of the flower. On the back, bend the ends of the wires away from the centre and secure.

Lacy surrounds

Transfer three large shapes and two small shapes to the water-soluble fabric and place it in the smaller hoop. On one shape, embroider chain stitch along the centre line and side branches. Ensure the side branches connect to the centre line.

Stitch four ghiordes knots along the centre line and two on each side branch. Embroider the four remaining shapes in the same manner. Cut the loops on the larger shapes to approximately 2cm (3/4") and the loops on the smaller shapes to approximately 1.5cm (5/8"). Cut out each shape and individually rinse each one until the fabric dissolves. Separate the threads. Spread the small shapes over the two marbles and the larger shapes over the backs of spoons. Leave until dry.

Attach the ends of the three large shapes under the petals of the flower. Secure the ends of the two smaller pieces to the position for the seedpod.

Seedpod

Cut a length of thread 1m (39 1/2") long. Leaving a 12cm (5") tail, wrap the thread twice around a skewer to form a small ring. Work detached blanket stitch over the ring to form a couronne. Remove from the skewer. Insert the point of the skewer into the bead and position the couronne on top of the bead. Work rows of detached blanket stitch until the bead is completely covered, increasing and decreasing the number of stitches in each row to fit the shape of the bead.

When reaching the base of the bead, secure the last stitch with two tiny back stitches. Do not cut off the excess thread.

Take the tails of thread back through the centre of the bead and to the back of the fabric at the marked position. Secure the tails firmly on the back of the fabric.

EMBROIDERY KEY

All embroidery is worked with one strand of thread unless otherwise specified.

Stems and surface embroidered leaves

Main stem = C
(2 strands, whipped chain stitch)

Leaf stems = C
(2 strands, whipped chain stitch)

Leaf outlines = D
(2 strands, chain stitch)

Leaf filling = D (2 strands, detached blanket stitch)

Leaf veins = E (straight stitch)

Detached leaves

Outlines = D (couching, 2 strands, chain stitch, blanket stitch)

Filling = D
(2 strands, detached blanket stitch)

Tendrils

Cut three pieces of green wire, each 7cm (2 3/4") long. Wrap each piece with the lightest green thread. Coil each piece of covered wire around the long darner. Sink the ends of the wire at the marked positions on the main stem and secure. Couch the tendrils in 1 - 2 places to ensure they stay in position.

Veins = E (straight stitch)

Stems = C (2 strands, wrapping)

Flower

Outer petals = B (couching, 3 strands, satin stitch, blanket stitch)

Veins of outer petals = B
(stem stitch)

Inner petals = A (couching, 3 strands, satin stitch, blanket stitch)

Veins of inner petals = A
(stem stitch)

Centre = A and F
(2 strands, ghiordes knot)

Stamens = E (2 strands, wrapping)

Lacy surrounds = E (2 strands, chain stitch, ghiordes knot)

Seed pod = D
(2 strands, detached blanket stitch)

Tendrils = E
(2 strands, wrapping, couching)

- TULIPA -

MATERIALS

Threads and needles

Au Ver à Soie, Soie d'Alger
A = 2115 dark grass green
B = 2215 dark khaki green
C = 3425 dark silver green
D = 4624 dark strawberry
E = 4625 very dark strawberry

DMC soft tapestry cotton
F = 2421 tan

Madeira no. 3 metallic thread
G = 3003 gold

Benton and Johnson no.6 smooth passing thread
H = gold 3m (3yd 10")

Benton and Johnson no. 9 bright check purl
I = gold 50cm (20")

Gütermann polyester machine sewing thread
J = 968 mustard

No. 10 crewel needle
No. 10 beading needle
No. 18 chenille needle

THIS DESIGN USES

Buttonhole stitch, Chipping, Couching, Long and short stitch
Long and short buttonhole stitch, Overcast stitch, Split back stitch
Stab stitch, Wirework

Supplies

Main fabric

Backing fabric

Gold kid 5cm (2") square

Gold felt 5cm (2") square

Burgundy homespun
23cm (9") square

Green homespun 18cm (7") square

1.1m (1yd 7 1/4") no. 30 gauge
white covered wire

Beeswax

Embroidery hoop
10cm (4") diameter

Embroidery hoop
15cm (6") diameter

Embroidery hoop
25cm (10") diameter

ORDER OF WORK

Use the chenille needle when laying threads and sinking wires, the beading needle for attaching the check purl and the crewel needle for all other embroidery.

Transfer the design using your chosen method and mount the main fabric in the largest hoop.

Tulips

Stems

Cut five lengths of soft tapestry cotton 10cm (4") longer than one stem. Pass them through the beeswax until they hold together or squeak. Run your fingers down the threads to remove any excess wax.

Beginning at the lower edge, couch the bundle of soft cotton along the stem outline. Take the ends of the cotton to the back of the fabric and secure. Completely cover with overcast stitch. Create the second stem in the same manner.

Leaves on main fabric

Transfer two leaf curl shapes to the gold felt and cut out. Attach them to the main fabric with stab stitches. Couch passing thread for the centre veins, placing the stitches 5mm (3/16") apart.

Outline the leaves with split back stitch and then fill in the lower sections of each leaf with long and short stitch.

Cut the check purl into chips 3 - 4mm (1/8 - 3/16") long. Using a waxed length of machine sewing thread, attach the pieces to the upper section of each leaf to form the leaf curls.

Detached leaf

Place the green homespun in the smallest hoop and transfer the leaf shape. Cut a 20cm (8") length of wire. Beginning and ending at the base of the leaf and using stitches approximately 1cm (3/8") apart, couch the wire around the leaf shape *(diag 1)*.

Diag 1

Embroider buttonhole stitches over the wire to completely cover it. Work a row of split back stitch just inside the buttonhole stitching and two rows across the base of the leaf between the wires.

Couch the centre vein in the same manner as the previous leaves. Beginning at the tip and covering the split back stitch, fill the leaf with long and short stitch. Carefully cut out the leaf and set it aside.

Petals on main fabric

Transfer the petal shapes to the wrong side of the gold kid and cut out. Attach to the main fabric in the same manner as the felt shapes.

Outline the petal of the uppermost tulip with split back stitch, except for the section that adjoins the gold petal. Using the lighter shade at the top and the darker shade near the base, fill the petal with long and short stitch.

On the lower tulip, complete the petal to the right of the gold petal first, stitching it in the same manner as the embroidered petal on the uppermost tulip. Work split back stitch around the entire outline of the petal on the left and fill in as before.

Detached petals

Place the burgundy homespun in the medium hoop and transfer the petal shapes. Cut six pieces of wire, each 14cm (5 1/2") long.

Beginning and ending at the base, couch a length of wire in place around each centre petal *(diag 2)*.

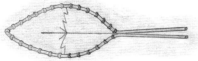

Diag 2

Keep the stitches approximately 2mm (^{1}/16") apart and use the darker shade of thread for the lower half of the petal and the lighter shade for the upper half. Repeat for the side petals, leaving a tiny tail of wire on one side *(diag 3)*.

Diag 3

Work a row of split back stitch just inside the wire, changing thread colour as before. Using long and short buttonhole stitches, cover the wire and split back stitch. Fill in the petal with long and short stitch.

Embroider the remaining petals in the same manner. Carefully cut out the petals and set them aside.

Scroll work

Embroider along each line with split back stitch, leaving spaces where a line is overlapped by another line. Couch passing thread alongside each line of split back stitch.

Applying the detached petals and leaf

Using the chenille needle, sink the wires of the centre petal on the uppermost tulip. Secure the wires on the back of the fabric. Trim the short tail of wire from two side petals. Sink the remaining wire on each petal in the same manner as before and secure. Make a small couching stitch approximately halfway along the outer edge of each side petal to hold them in place. Trim the tails of wire on the back of the fabric and shape the petals by placing your finger inside the flower and moulding the petals around it. Repeat the procedure for the second tulip.

Sink each wire on the leaf separately and secure on the back of the fabric. Secure the base of the leaf to the fabric with tiny stitches. Trim off excess wire. Gently stroke the leaf to shape it.

EMBROIDERY KEY

All embroidery is worked with one strand of thread unless otherwise specified.

Tulips

Petals on main fabric

Gold petals = J (stab stitch)

Outlines of red petals = D (split back stitch)

Filling of red petals = D and E (long and short stitch)

Detached petals

Outlines = D and E (couching, split back stitch, long and short buttonhole stitch)

Filling = D and E (long and short stitch)

Stems = F (5 lengths, padding), A (couching, overcast stitch)

Leaves on main fabric

Outlines = C (split back stitch)

Filling = C (long and short stitch)

Centre veins = H (laid thread), G (couching)

Leaf curls = I (chipping)

Detached leaf

Outlines = C (couching, buttonhole stitch, split back stitch)

Filling = C (long and short stitch)

Centre veins = H (laid thread), G (couching)

Scroll work = B (split back stitch), H (laid thread), G (couching)

by Annette Rich

- GERALDTON WAX -

MATERIALS

Threads and needles

Edmar Glory fine 2 ply rayon thread

A = 8 variegated lemon
B = 41 shaded antique mauve
C = 45 variegated moss rock
D = 53 shaded lime

No. 6 crewel needle
No. 8 straw (milliner's) needle
Long darner

Supplies

Main fabric

Backing fabric

Pale pink homespun
15cm (6") square

Lightweight fusible interfacing
15cm (6") square

White machine sewing thread

112.5cm (45") no. 30 gauge white
covered wire

Embroidery hoop
10cm (4") diameter

Embroidery hoop
15cm (6") diameter

THIS DESIGN USES

Bullion knot, Circular Rhodes stitch, Couching, French knot
Granitos, Overcast stitch, Padded satin stitch, Satin stitch, Stem stitch
Split stitch, Straight stitch, Wirework

ORDER OF WORK

Use the long darner for sinking the wires, the straw needle for working the bullion knots and couching, and the crewel needle for all other embroidery.

Transfer the design using your chosen method and mount the main fabric in the larger hoop.

Surface embroidery

Stitch a granitos for each bud. Work all stems with a single row of stem stitch, adding a French knot to the base of each bud as you reach them. Add a second row of stem stitch to the base of the main stem.

Embroider the centre of each blossom with circular Rhodes stitch. Next, work the padded satin stitch petals of the six flowers on the main fabric. Outline each petal with split stitch and then work three chain stitches across the petal inside the outline. Work satin stitches lengthwise over the petal. Surround the petal with a bullion knot and couch in place. Add a French knot at the base of each petal for stamens.

Stitch the fronds next. Begin by working a long straight stitch stem and couching it in place. Add straight stitches to the stem, angling them slightly towards the tip.

Detached flowers

Fuse the interfacing to the wrong side of the pink fabric. Mount in the smaller hoop. Transfer five large petal shapes and ten small ones to the right side of the fabric.

Cut fifteen lengths of wire, each 7.5cm (3") long. Bend one piece of wire to fit a petal shape. Using the white machine sewing thread, couch the wire to the outline. Change to the mauve thread and overcast the wire to the fabric around the petal shape.

Pad the petal and cover with satin stitch in the same manner as the petals on the main fabric *(diag 1).* Work all remaining petals in the same manner. Carefully cut out all the petals.

Diag 1

Assembling the detached flowers

Using the long darner, insert the wires for one petal into the main fabric at the required position. Secure the wires on the back of the fabric. Repeat the procedure for all remaining petals.

To finish, add a French knot at the base of each petal for stamens.

EMBROIDERY KEY

All embroidery is worked with one strand of thread unless otherwise specified.

Surface embroidery

Flowers

Centre = A
(circular Rhodes stitch)

Petals = B
(split stitch, padded satin stitch)

Petal outlines = B
(bullion knot, 35 - 40 wraps, couching)

Stamens = C (French knot, 2 wraps)

Buds

Petals = B (granitos)

Calyxes = C (French knot, 1 wrap)

Stems and leaves

Main stem = C (stem stitch)

Fronds = D
(straight stitch, couching)

Detached flowers

Centre = A (circular Rhodes stitch)

Petals = B (satin stitch)

Petal outlines = B (overcast stitch)

Stamens = C
(French knot, 2 wraps)

- CHRISTMAS BELLS -

THIS DESIGN USES

Beading, Blanket stitch, Chain stitch

Couching, Detached chain

Long and short stitch

Overcast stitch, Padded satin stitch

Satin stitch, Split stitch

Straight stitch, Wirework

MATERIALS

Threads, beads and needles

Edmar Ciré heavy
3 ply rayon thread
A = 9 shaded tangerine
B = 69 shaded daffodil
C = 121 pistachio green
D = 200 Christmas red
E = 225 camel
F = 305 overdyed grey-green
G = 317 overdyed lichen

Edmar Glory fine
2 ply rayon thread
H = 225 camel

Mill Hill glass seed beads
I = 00557 gold

Mill Hill small bugle beads
6mm (¹/₄″) long
J = 72053 nutmeg

No. 5 crewel needle

No. 9 beading needle

Long darner

Supplies

Main fabric

Backing fabric

White homespun
25cm (10") square

Lightweight fusible interfacing
25cm (10") square

White machine sewing thread

30cm (12") no. 30 gauge white
covered wire

Embroidery hoop 10cm (4")
diameter

Embroidery hoop 20cm (8")
diameter

ORDER OF WORK

Use the long darner for sinking the
wires, the beading needle for
attaching the beads and the crewel
needle for all other embroidery.

Transfer the design using your
chosen method and mount the
main fabric in the larger hoop.

Embroidery on main fabric

Grass and stems

Work a line of chain stitch along
each blade of grass for padding.
Cover the chain stitch with angled
satin stitches, using the same thread
colour as the chain stitch. Embroider
the two stems in the same manner.

Bud

Outline the bud with split stitch and
fill with chain stitch for padding.
Cover the padding and outline with
angled satin stitches.

Back sections of detached bells

Stitch the lower edge with blanket
stitch. Fill the inside of the bells
with satin stitch.

Bells on main fabric

Embroider the rim of each flower
with blanket stitch and the inside of
the petals with satin stitch. Work a
split stitch outline along each side
of the two flowers. Stitching from
the base to the rim, fill the petals
with long and short stitch. Using the
paler sections of the thread, add
three long straight stitches to each
flower for petal markings.

Sepals

Add the sepals to the base of the
bud and the left bell embroidered
on the main fabric. For each sepal,
stitch three detached chains. Start
each stitch from the same hole in
the fabric and work the shortest
detached chain first, then the
medium one and finally the longest.

Detached flowers

Fuse the interfacing to the wrong
side of the white fabric and mount
the fabric in the smaller hoop.
Transfer the flower shapes to the
right side of the fabric.

Cut three pieces of wire, each 10cm
(4") long. Bend one piece of wire to
fit the lower edge of one petal.
Using the white machine sewing
thread, couch the wire to the
outline. Completely cover the wired
edge with overcast stitch.

RAMPION BELLFLOWER
campanula rapuncuoides

GIANT BELLFLOWER
campanula latifolia

PEACH BELLFLOWER
campanula persicifolia

Directly above the wire, embroider a row of long and short stitch with the daffodil thread. Change to the red thread and continue in long and short stitch until approximately two thirds of the shape is covered. Embroider the two remaining flowers in the same manner.

Attaching to the main fabric

Carefully cut out one flower, leaving a 3mm (¹/₈") seam allowance along the unwired edges. Sink the wires into the main fabric at the required position but do not secure. Turn under the seam allowance and stitch the slip to the main fabric along the unwired edges. Fill the upper third of the slip with long and short stitch, stitching through both the slip and the main fabric. Secure the wires on the back of the fabric.

Place a finger inside the bell to hold the shape and add straight stitch markings in the same manner as those on the bells embroidered on the main fabric. Repeat the procedure for all remaining petals.

Stamens

Using doubled thread, slip a bugle bead and then a seed bead onto the needle. Take the thread back through the bugle bead only. Leaving tails of thread approximately 5cm (2") long, tie the two tails together at the end of the bugle bead. Make eight more stamens in the same manner. Thread the tails of one stamen into the needle. Take the needle to the back of the fabric under the raised petals. Check the stamen is hanging at the desired length and then secure the thread on the back of the fabric. Attach the remaining stamens in the same manner.

EMBROIDERY KEY

All embroidery is worked with one strand of thread unless otherwise specified.

Christmas bells

Flowers on main fabric

Outlines = D (split stitch)

Outside of petals = D (long and short stitch)

Inside of petals = A (satin stitch)

Rim = B (blanket stitch)

Petal markings = A (straight stitch)

Detached flowers

Outside of petals = D (long and short stitch)

Inside of petals = A (satin stitch)

Rim = B (overcast stitch, long and short stitch), machine sewing thread (couching)

Petal markings = A (straight stitch)

Stamens = H, I and J (2 strands, beading)

Bud = B and D (chain stitch, padded satin stitch)

Sepals = F (detached chain)

Stems = E (chain stitch, padded satin stitch)

Grass = C, F and G (chain stitch, padded satin stitch)

The Magical Pomegranate, *Inspirations* issue 39

Wild Thing, *Inspirations* issue 42

by Alison Cole

- SPRING SPLENDOUR -

MATERIALS

Threads and needles

Au Ver à Soie, Soie d'Alger
A = 2115 dark grass green
B = 2215 dark khaki green
C = 3425 dark silver-green
D = 4634 medium grey-mauve
E = 4635 dark grey-mauve
F = 4636 very dark grey-mauve

DMC soft tapestry cotton
G = 2421 tan

Madeira no. 3 metallic thread
H = 3003 gold

Benton and Johnson no. 6 smooth passing thread
I = gold 3m (3yd 10")

Benton and Johnson no. 9 bright check purl
J = gold 50cm (20")

Gütermann polyester machine sewing thread
K = 968 mustard

No. 10 crewel needle
No. 10 beading needle
No. 18 chenille needle

Supplies

Main fabric

Backing fabric

Gold kid 5cm (2") square

Gold felt 5cm (2") square

Antique lavender homespun 23cm (9") square

Green homespun 23cm (9") square

1.15m (1yd 9 1/4") no. 30 gauge white covered wire

Beeswax

Embroidery hoop 25cm (10") diameter

Embroidery hoop 15cm (6") diameter

ORDER OF WORK

Use the chenille needle when laying threads and sinking wires, the beading needle for attaching the check purl and the crewel needle for all other embroidery.

Transfer the design using your chosen method and mount the main fabric in the larger hoop.

Irises

Stems

Cut five lengths of soft tapestry cotton 10cm (4") longer than the stems. Pass them through the beeswax until they hold together or squeak. Run your fingers down the threads to remove any excess wax.

Beginning at the lower edge, couch the bundle of soft cotton along the stem. Take the ends of the cotton to

the back of the fabric and secure. Completely cover with overcast stitch.

Leaves on main fabric

Transfer two leaf curl shapes to the gold felt and cut out. Attach the shapes to the main fabric with stab stitches.

Outline the leaf with split back stitch and then fill in the lower sections of each leaf with long and short stitch.

Cut the check purl into chips 3 - 4mm (1/8 - 3/16") long. Using a waxed length of machine sewing thread, attach the pieces to the upper section of each leaf to form the leaf curls.

Detached leaf

Place the green homespun in the smaller hoop and transfer the leaf shape. Cut a 25cm (10") length of wire.

Beginning and ending at the base of the leaf and using stitches 1cm (3/8") apart, couch the wire in place

around the shape. Embroider buttonhole stitches over the wire to completely cover it and then a row of split back stitch just inside the buttonhole edging.

Beginning at the tip and covering the split back stitch, fill the leaf with long and short stitch. Carefully cut out the leaf and set it aside.

Petals on main fabric

Transfer the petal shapes to the back of the gold kid and cut out. Attach them to the main fabric in the same manner as the felt leaf shapes.

Outline the lower side petals on each flower with split back stitch. Fill each petal with long and short stitch, covering the outline.

Detached petals

Place the antique lavender homespun in the smaller hoop and transfer the petal shapes. Cut six pieces of wire, each 15cm (6") long.

Beginning and ending at the base of one middle petal, couch a length of wire around the shape *(diag 1)*.

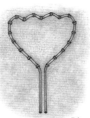

Diag 1

Cover the wire with closely packed buttonhole stitches and then work a row of split back stitch just inside. Fill in the petal with long and short stitch, covering the split back stitch.

Using the lightest shade of mauve, couch a wire around one upper petal. Cover the wire with buttonhole stitch and then work a row of split back stitch just inside. Work long and short stitch across the upper edge and halfway down the sides with the same shade of thread. Change to the middle shade and fill in the remaining upper half. Fill the remaining space with the darkest shade of thread. Stitch a second petal in the same manner. Embroider the petals for the remaining iris in the same manner. Carefully cut out the petals and set them aside.

Beard

Cut a 3cm (1 ⅛") length of check purl and stretch it out until it is almost straight. Scrunch it up and rub it between the palms of your hands until it is a matted bundle. This will be attached to the upper iris after the detached petals are applied.

Cut a 2cm (¾") length of check purl and make the beard for the lower iris in the same manner.

Scroll work

Embroider along each line with split back stitch, leaving spaces where a line is overlapped by another line. Couch passing thread alongside each line of split back stitch.

Applying the detached petals and leaf

Petals

Trim the short tails of wire from the upper petals. Using the chenille needle, sink the wires of the upper petals just below the gold kid petal, using the same hole in the fabric for both petals. Secure the wires on the back of the fabric. Sink the wires of the centre petal just below the previous two. Trim the tails of wire. Mould the petals around your finger to shape them. Repeat the procedure for the second iris.

Beard

Position the beard for the upper iris onto the middle petal. Using waxed machine sewing thread and small stitches, secure the base of the beard to the centre of the flower. With a finger beneath the petal for support, press the beard onto the petal to mould it to the petal shape. Attach the beard to the lower iris in the same manner.

Leaf

Sink the wires and fold them on the back of the fabric along the stem. Secure the wires and trim off the excess. Gently stroke the leaf to shape it.

EMBROIDERY KEY

All embroidery is worked with one strand of thread unless otherwise specified.

Irises

Petals on main fabric

Gold petal = K (stab stitch)

Outlines of lower side petals = F (split back stitch)

Filling of lower side petals = F (long and short stitch)

Detached petals

Outline of centre petal = F (couching, split back stitch, buttonhole stitch)

Filling of centre petal = F (long and short stitch)

Outline of upper petals = D (couching, split back stitch, buttonhole stitch)

Filling of upper petals = D, E and F (long and short stitch)

Beard = J

Stems = G (5 strands, padding), A (couching, overcast stitch)

Leaves on main fabric

Outlines = C (split back stitch)

Filling = C (long and short stitch)

Leaf curls = J (chipping)

Detached leaf

Outlines = C (couching, buttonhole stitch, split back stitch)

Filling = C (long and short stitch)

Scroll work = A (split back stitch), I (laid thread), H (couching)

by Wendy Innes

- GOSSAMER -

THIS DESIGN USES

Beading, Blanket stitch
Couching, Stab stitch
Straight stitch, Wirework

MATERIALS

Threads, beads and needles

DMC stranded cotton
A = blanc

DMC stranded rayon
B = 30504 very light blue-green

Kreinik metallic cable thread
C = 001P silver

Kreinik no. 1 Japanese thread
D = 001J silver

Kreinik no. 7 Japanese thread
E = 001J silver

Benton and Johnson no. 1 pearl purl
F = silver 1.15m (1yd 5")

Benton and Johnson no. 3 pearl purl
G = silver 5cm (2")

Benton and Johnson super pearl purl
H = silver 90cm (35 1/2")

Benton and Johnson bright check purl
I = silver 30cm (12")

Gütermann polyester machine sewing thread
J = 800 white

Mill Hill petite glass beads
K = 42010 ice

Mill Hill glass treasures
L = 12031 small marbled opal bell flower x 5

Faceted glass bead 5mm (3/16")
M = crystal

No. 10 beading needle
No. 10 crewel needle
No. 18 chenille needle

Supplies

Main fabric

Backing fabric

White taffeta
15cm x 30cm wide (6" x 12")

White broadcloth 18cm (7") square

Silver lamé 5cm (2") square

Matte silver kid
3cm x 10cm wide (1 1/4" x 4")

Shiny silver kid 5cm (2") square

Fusible webbing 5cm (2") square

2 x 7mm (5/16") crystal rhinestones

10 x 4mm (3/16") crystal rhinestones

2.2m (2yd 14 1/2") no. 28 gauge uncovered wire

Small amount of polyester fibre-fill

White PVA glue

Embroidery hoop
10cm (4") diameter

Embroidery hoop
13cm (5") diameter

Embroidery hoop
25cm (10") diameter

ORDER OF WORK

Use the chenille needle when laying threads and sinking wires, the beading needle for attaching the check purl and the crewel needle for all other embroidery.

Transfer the design using your chosen method and mount the main fabric in the largest hoop.

Butterfly

Wings

Cut the taffeta into two 15cm (6") squares. Transfer one upper and one lower wing shape to one piece of fabric and mount it in the smallest hoop. Cut two lengths of wire, one 25cm (10") long and the other 15cm (6") long. Leaving two tails of wire, shape and couch the longer wire to the upper wing. Cover the wire with blanket stitch. Shape and attach the shorter wire to the lower wing in the same manner.

Stitch the lines on both wings with long straight stitches.

Transfer the wing markings to the wrong side of the shiny silver kid and cut out. Using stab stitch, secure a piece to each wing at the marked position. Couch pearl purl along both sides of the kid and on top of the blanket stitch around the outer edges of the wings.

Glue one large rhinestone and five small rhinestones to the upper wing at the marked positions. Allow the glue to dry completely. Couch pearl purl around each rhinestone, bringing the thread to the front on the outside of the purl and taking it to the back of the fabric against the rhinestone.

Carefully cut out the wings and set them aside. Repeat the procedure for the remaining two wings.

Using the chenille needle, sink the wires for the lower wings at the positions indicated. Secure the tails of wire on the back of the fabric. Repeat for the upper wings.

Body

Transfer the body shape to the wrong side of the matte silver kid and cut out. Position the kid on the fabric (it will just cover the edge of the upper wings). Attach with small stab stitches, leaving a small opening. Insert fibre-fill through the opening and then stitch it closed. Outline the body with couched pearl purl and attach a short length of check purl across the body to separate the thorax from the abdomen. Attach the crystal bead for the head and then couch down super pearl purl for the tail and antennae.

Lily of the valley

Leaves

Mount the broadcloth into the medium hoop and transfer the leaf shapes. Cut two pieces of wire, each 30cm (12") long.

Beginning at the tip on one leaf, couch the wire along the centre vein and then around the outer edge of the leaf. Work blanket stitch around the outer edge, covering the wire.

Cut a 1m (39 1/2") length of thread and fold in half. Starting at the tip of

the leaf, lay the thread alongside the centre vein and couch in place with stitches approximately 5mm (3/16") apart. When reaching the base of the leaf, crimp the thread and couch towards the tip again, placing the couching stitches so they form a brickwork pattern. Continue couching lengths of thread in the same manner until this half of the leaf is filled. Repeat for the remaining half.

Couch pearl purl around the leaf in the same manner as the wings. Carefully remove the couching stitches from the wire along the centre vein and lift the wire slightly. Cut a length of pearl purl the same length as the vein and slide it over the wire. Reposition the vein and couch it in place.

Make a second leaf following the same procedure. Carefully cut out the leaves and set them aside.

Flowers and stems

Cut two pieces of wire, each 15cm (6") long and three pieces, each

10cm (4") long. Transfer five sepal shapes to the fusible webbing and fuse it to the wrong side of the silver lamé. Cut out the sepals.

Thread three beads onto one length of wire. Twist the end around the wire just above the beads *(diag 1)*. Thread a bell onto the wire and then a 12mm (1/2") length of super pearl purl. Secure the base of one sepal to the wire just below the pearl purl. Take care not to get any kinks in the wire.

Diag 1

Fashion four more flowers and stems in the same manner.

Cut a 5cm (2") length of pearl purl for the main stem. Slide one of the longer flower stems inside the main stem. Approximately 6mm (1/4") from the top of the main stem, make a slight kink in the pearl purl. At this point, insert the remaining long flower stem into the main stem. Insert the three remaining flower stems in the same manner spacing them approximately 7mm (5/16") apart.

Attaching the leaves and stem

Using the chenille needle, sink the wires for the leaves at the positions indicated. Secure the tails of wire on the back of the fabric. Shape the leaves and couch the tip of each one to the main fabric.

Sink and secure the wires at the base of the main stem in the same manner. Couch the main stem to

Gossamer

the leaf and shape the flower stems. Trim the excess wire on the back of the fabric.

Spider web

Secure the thread to the edge of the right hand leaf and thread a bead onto the needle. Slide the bead along the thread until it is approximately 2cm (³/₄") from the leaf. Take the needle back through the bead and pull firmly to prevent the bead from sliding. Take the thread through the fabric at the base of the web and re-emerge at the base of the second strand of the web. Attach two beads in the same manner as before. Take the thread through the leaf and attach three beads before anchoring the thread at the base on the back of the fabric.

Foreground

Cut the check purl into short pieces of varying lengths. Secure the pieces to the fabric in the same manner as attaching a bead.

EMBROIDERY KEY

All embroidery is worked with one strand of thread unless otherwise specified.

Butterfly

Upper wings

Attaching wire = A (couching, blanket stitch)

Attaching markings = A (stab stitch)

Wing outlines = J (couching), F (laid thread)

Line markings = C (straight stitch)

Spots = crystal rhinestones

Spot and marking outlines = J (couching), H (laid thread)

Lower wings

Attaching wire = A (couching, blanket stitch)

Attaching markings = A (stab stitch)

Wing outlines = J (couching), F (laid thread)

Marking outlines = J (couching), H (laid thread)

Line markings = C (straight stitch)

Body

Attaching body = J (stab stitch)

Body outline = J (couching), F (laid thread)

Head = M (beading)

Division between thorax and abdomen = I (beading)

Tail and antennae = J (couching), H (laid thread)

Lily of the valley

Leaves

Attaching wire = A (couching, blanket stitch)

Outline = J (couching), F (laid thread)

Centre vein = J (couching), F (laid thread)

Filling = B (couching), E (laid thread)

Flowers and stems

Main stem = J (couching), G (laid thread)

Flower stems = H

Flowers = L

Stamens = K

Sepals = silver lamé fabric

Spider web

Web = D (straight stitch)

Dewdrops = K (beading)

Foreground = I (beading)

Monarch, *Inspirations* issue 42

- SPIRIT OF SPRING -

THIS DESIGN USES

Back stitch, Beading, Buttonhole stitch, Couching, Long and short stitch

Overcast stitch, Single feather stitch, Split back stitch, Stab stitch

Straight stitch, Whipped chain stitch, Wirework

MATERIALS

Threads, beads and needles

Au Ver à Soie, Soie d'Alger
A = 2215 dark khaki green
B = 2932 light dusty rose
C = 2933 dusty rose
D = 2934 medium dusty rose
E = 3425 dark silver-green

Madeira stranded silk
F = 2008 mahogany

Madeira no. 3 metallic thread
G = 3003 gold

Madeira no. 40 metallic thread
H = 482 sunset

Benton and Johnson no. 6 smooth passing thread
I = gold 2m (2yd 7")

Benton and Johnson no. 9 bright check purl
J = gold 20cm (8")

Benton and Johnson super pearl purl
K = gold 20cm (8")

Mettler silky sheen machine sewing thread
L = 932 copper

Gütermann polyester machine sewing thread
M = 968 mustard

Mill Hill glass seed beads
N = 00330 copper

Mill Hill size 6 bead
O = 16025 wildberry

No. 10 crewel needle
No. 10 beading needle
No. 18 chenille needle
No. 28 tapestry needle

Supplies

Main fabric

Backing fabric

Gold kid 5cm (2") square

Gold felt 5cm (2") square

Pink homespun 23cm (9") square

Green homespun 23cm (9") square

Burgundy crystal organza 18cm (7") square

Gold glass organza 18cm (7") square

Fusible webbing 14cm (5 1/2") square

75cm (29 1/2") no. 30 gauge white covered wire

36cm (14") no. 28 gauge uncovered wire

Beeswax

Embroidery hoop 13cm (5") diameter

Embroidery hoop 15cm (6") diameter

Embroidery hoop 25cm (10") diameter

ORDER OF WORK

Use the chenille needle when laying threads and sinking wires, the beading needle for attaching the check purl and beads, the tapestry needle for whipping and the crewel needle for all other embroidery.

Transfer the design using your chosen method and mount the main fabric in the largest hoop.

Waterlily

Leaves on main fabric

Outline the two leaves, except where they touch the petals, with split back stitch. Fill the leaves with long and short stitch.

Detached leaf

Place the green homespun in the medium hoop and transfer the leaf shape. Cut a 15cm (6") length of covered wire.

Beginning and ending at the base of the leaf and using stitches 1cm (3/8") apart, couch the wire around the leaf shape *(diag 1)*.

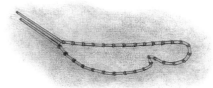

Diag 1

Embroider buttonhole stitches over the wire to completely cover it.

Work a row of split back stitch just inside the buttonhole stitching and two rows across the base of the leaf between the wires. Fill the leaf with long and short stitch. Carefully cut out the leaf and set it aside.

Petals on main fabric

Transfer the petal shapes to the wrong side of the gold kid and cut out. Attach them to the main fabric with waxed thread and stab stitches.

Outline the remaining five petals with split back stitch, following the diagram *(diag 2)*.

Diag 2

Using the lightest shade of pink near the tip and grading to the darkest shade at the base, fill each petal with long and short stitch.

Detached petals

Place the pink homespun in the medium hoop and transfer the petal shapes. Cut six pieces of covered wire, each 10cm (4") long.

Beginning and ending at the base of one petal, couch a length of wire in place around the shape *(diag 3)*.

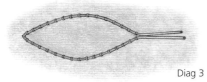

Diag 3

Embroider over the wire with buttonhole stitch and then work a row of split back stitch just inside it. Fill the petal with long and short stitch in the same manner as the petals on the main fabric.

Stitch the remaining petals in the same manner. Carefully cut out the petals and set them aside.

Scroll work

Embroider along each line with split back stitch, leaving spaces where a line is overlapped by another line. Couch passing thread alongside each line of split back stitch.

Dragonfly

Thorax

Transfer the two padding shapes to the gold felt and cut out. Attach the smaller shape to the main fabric in the middle of the thorax using stab stitch. Place the larger felt piece over the first and attach in the same manner.

Transfer the thorax shape to the wrong side of the gold kid and cut out. Attach it to the main fabric with waxed thread and stab stitches.

Detached wings

Fuse the gold glass organza to the burgundy crystal organza with the fusible webbing. Place the gold organza on a different angle to the burgundy organza *(diag 4)*.

Diag 4

Mount the fabric in the smallest hoop and transfer the wing shapes. Cut two pieces of uncovered wire, each 18cm (7") long. Shape and couch the wires to the wing outlines. Work overcast stitch along each wire. At the base of each wing, work five overcast stitches over both wires. Leave the thread dangling, this will be used to attach the wings later.

Embroider the wing markings with two rows of single feather stitch.

Cut out the wings, knot the dangling thread around the wires at the base of each wing and set them aside.

Wings on main fabric

Using the excess unfused organza from the detached wings, place the two layers of fabric over one wing shape on the main fabric. Stitch over the wing outline with very tiny split back stitches. Cut away the excess organza level with the stitching. Repeat for the remaining wing.

Cut a 10cm (4") length of pearl purl. Stretch it until it is approximately 15cm (6") long. Couch the pearl purl over the split back stitch outline. Embroider the wing markings in the same manner as the detached wings. Repeat for the remaining wing.

Abdomen and legs

Beginning at the thorax, work a row of chain stitch to the tip of the abdomen. Work a second row of chain stitch from the thorax to approximately three-quarters of the way to the end. Again beginning at the thorax, whip the two rows together. Continue whipping the single row of chain stitch to the end.

Using the photograph as a guide to stitch placement, embroider each leg with three back stitches. Work two straight stitches in a 'V' shape at the end of the abdomen.

Applying the detached pieces

Petals and leaf

Trim the short tail of wire from the petals. Beginning from the centre and working towards the sides, sink the wires of the petals. Secure the wires on the back of the fabric.

Sink each wire on the leaf separately and secure on the back of the fabric. Secure the base of the leaf to the fabric with tiny stitches.

Shape the petals by placing your finger inside the flower and moulding the petals around it. Repeat for the leaf.

Trim the tails of wire on the back of the fabric.

Stamens

Cut fourteen pieces of check purl. Vary the length of the pieces from 5 - 12mm (3/16 - 1/2"). Using waxed thread, attach eight pieces to the centre of the flower in the same way that you attach a bead. The remaining six pieces are attached so they stand up. To do this, follow the instructions for attaching a bead to the end of a bead on page 41, using a tiny chip of check purl instead of the second bead. Repeat for the remaining stamens.

EMBROIDERY KEY

All embroidery is worked with one strand of thread unless otherwise specified.

Waterlily

Petals on main fabric

Gold petals = M (stab stitch)

Outlines of pink petals = B (split back stitch)

Filling of pink petals = B, C and D (long and short stitch)

Detached petals

Outlines = C (couching, split back stitch, buttonhole stitch)

Filling = B, C and D (long and short stitch)

Stamens = J and M (beading)

Leaves on main fabric

Outlines = E (split back stitch)

Filling = E (long and short stitch)

Dragonfly wings, head and eyes

Sink the wires of the wings just above the thorax and secure them on the back of the fabric with the dangling threads.

Using the same thread, attach the large bead just below the thorax. Take the thread through the bead twice and then thread the two seed beads onto the needle. Take the needle back through the large bead and to the back of the fabric. Secure the thread on the back of the fabric.

Detached leaf

Outlines = E (couching, buttonhole stitch, split back stitch)

Filling = E (long and short stitch)

Dragonfly

Detached wings

Outline = L (couching, overcast stitch)

Markings = G (single feather stitch)

Wings on main fabric

Outline = L (split back stitch), K (laid thread), M (couching)

Markings = G (single feather stitch)

Thorax = M (stab stitch)

Abdomen = F (2 strands, whipped chain stitch), H (straight stitch)

Legs = H (back stitch)

Head = O (beading)

Eyes = N (beading)

Scroll work = A (split back stitch), I (laid thread), G (couching)

- F O R B I D D E N   F R U I T -

THIS DESIGN USES

Bullion knot, Bullion loop, Chain stitch, Couching
Detached blanket stitch, Needlewoven bar, Needlewoven picot
Ribbon stitch, Stem stitch, Straight stitch, Trapunto
Wirework, Wrapping

MATERIALS

Threads, ribbons and needles

*Les Designs Creative Threads
'Virgolina' round rayon cord*
A = mystic indigo
B = evergreen

DMC broder médicis fine wool
C = 8204 beaver grey
D = 8405 light sage
E = 8611 dark camel

DMC no. 8 perlé cotton
F = 3743 very light antique violet

Au Ver à Soie, chenille à broder
G = 3322 light silver purple
H = 3413 grey taupe
I = 5116 very dark dusky violet

*House of Embroidery hand dyed
perlé cotton*
J = 56 holly

Madeira stranded metallic thread
K = 5014 black-gold

*Mokuba no. 1500 organza ribbon
5mm (3/16") wide*
L = 2 white

*Machine sewing threads to match
rayon cords and chenille*

No. 9 crewel needle
No. 9 straw
(milliner's) needle
No. 18 chenille
needle
No. 24 tapestry
needle

Supplies

Main fabric

Backing fabric

15cm (6") no. 30 gauge green covered wire

Small amount of polyester fibre-fill

Embroidery hoop
15cm (6") diameter

ORDER OF WORK

Use the straw needle for working the bullion knots and loops, the chenille needle for the ribbon and laid threads, the tapestry needle for the needlelace and the crewel needle for all other embroidery.

Transfer the design using your chosen method. Mount both fabrics in the hoop.

Passionfruit

Beginning and ending at the top, couch the indigo cord along the outline of the fruit with matching machine sewing thread. Turn the fabric over to the wrong side. Make a small slit in the backing fabric only. Insert the polyester fibre-fill to lightly pad the fruit. Stitch the opening closed.

Flip the fabric over to the right side again. Working from the outer edge and spiralling towards the centre, completely cover the fruit with couched chenille threads.

Couch the green cord for the stem in place. At the lower end, work three rows of chain stitch to form the foundation of the sepals *(diag 1)*. Embroider a single row of detached blanket stitch into the outer rows of chain stitch. Work 2 - 3 rows on each side of the middle row of chain stitch.

Diag 1

Stitch two needlewoven picots between the sepals and the fruit for withered petals. Twist them before anchoring the ends. Add four needlewoven bars between the petals for withered stamens.

At the upper end of the stem, stitch two small leaves. Use two bullion knots for the leaf on the right and three for the leaf on the left. Embroider the tendril on the right hand side with stem stitch, adding two bullion loops towards the end. To make the tendril on the left, wrap the length of wire with green yarn. Coil the wire around the chenille needle. Remove the needle and attach each end of the coiled wire to the fabric.

Bees

Embroider the head and body of each bee with bullion knots positioned side by side. Alternate the two shades of yarn. To each bee, add two small straight stitches for the antennae and two pairs of ribbon stitches for the wings.

EMBROIDERY KEY

All thread embroidery is worked with one strand unless otherwise specified.

Passionfruit

Fruit

Outline = A (couching)

Filling = G, H and I (couching)

Sepals = J (chain stitch, detached blanket stitch)

Withered petals = E (needlewoven picot)

Withered stamens = F (needlewoven bar)

Stem, leaves and tendrils

Stem = B (couching)

Leaves = D
(2 - 3 bullion knots, 9 - 16 wraps)

Tendril on left = D (wrapping)

Tendril on right = D (stem stitch, bullion loop, 12 - 20 wraps)

Bees

Head and body = C and E
(8 - 9 bullion knots, 7 - 15 wraps)

Antennae = K (straight stitch)

Wings = L (ribbon stitch)

- VERITY -

MATERIALS

Threads and needles

DMC stranded cotton

A = 815 dark garnet
B = 817 very dark coral red
C = 970 light pumpkin
D = 3011 dark khaki green
E = 3051 dark green-grey

No. 10 crewel needle
No. 10 straw (milliner's) needle
Long darner

Supplies

Main fabric

Backing fabric

8 pieces of quilter's muslin, each 20cm (8") square

2.4m (2yd 22 1/2") no. 28 gauge uncovered wire

1 round bead 4mm (3/16") diameter

Embroidery hoop 10cm (4") diameter

Embroidery hoop 20cm (8") diameter

ORDER OF WORK

Use the straw needle for wrapping the bead, the long darner for sinking wires and the crewel needle for all other embroidery.

Mount the main fabric in the larger hoop and transfer the design using your chosen method.

Detached petals and leaf

All detached pieces are worked in the same manner.

Trace the four tiny petals onto the centre of a piece of muslin. Trace the three small petals onto a second piece, the three medium petals onto a third piece and the two large petals and the leaf onto a fourth piece.

Rose petals

Cut twelve lengths of wire, each approximately 18cm (7") long. Place an unmarked piece of muslin behind the piece with the four tiny petals marked on it and mount the two pieces together in the smaller hoop. Ensure the fabric is drum tight.

Beginning and ending at the base of one petal and using stitches approximately 1cm (3/8") apart, couch a piece of wire around the petal shape. Embroider closely packed blanket stitches over the wire to completely cover it.

Using the same thread, cover the top half of the petal with long and short stitch, starting at the outer edge and working towards the centre. Change to the darker shade of red and work the lower centre of the petal, blending the stitches into the previous shade. Embroider the remaining tiny petals in the same manner.

Repeat the procedure for the three small petals and three medium petals. Stitch the two large petals in the same manner, using the darkest shade of red to completely cover each one. Change to the lighter shade of red and add several straight stitch highlights over the previous stitching.

Leaf

Cut a piece of wire 20cm (8") long. Couch the wire around the outer edge of the leaf shape and along the centre vein. Work over-cast stitch along the centre vein and cover the outer edge of the leaf in the same manner as the petals. Fill each half with long and short stitch.

Stems

Beginning at the base of the stem and working to the base of the bud, embroider the main stem with padded satin stitch. Work the stems for the leaves and rose in the same manner. Stitch the new growth along the sides of the large leaf stem with satin stitch.

Bud

Outline the petals with split back stitch. Work horizontal satin stitch for padding and then cover with vertical satin stitch. Embroider the outline of the calyx and receptacle with split back stitch. Cover the calyx with long and short stitch and work the tiny section of calyx on the right hand side with straight stitch. Embroider the receptacle with padded satin stitch.

Leaves

Outline all the leaves on the main fabric with split back stitch.

Left hand side leaf

Starting at the tip and using the darker shade of green thread, embroider the lower half of the leaf

THIS DESIGN USES

Blanket stitch, Couching

Ghiordes knot

Long and short stitch

Overcast stitch

Padded satin stitch

Satin stitch, Split back stitch

Split stitch, Stem stitch

Straight stitch, Wirework

Wrapping

with long and short stitch. Angle the stitches towards the tip.

Using the lighter shade of green thread, work the upper half of the leaf in the same manner. Stitch the centre vein with split stitch and the leaf stem with stem stitch.

Lower right hand leaf

Embroider the upper half of the leaf in the same manner as the left hand leaf. Fill the lower half of the leaf with long and short stitch and then add the straight stitch highlights. Stitch the underside of the leaf with straight stitch. Work the centre vein in the same manner as before.

Centre right hand leaf

Using long and short stitch, work the lower side of the leaf with the lighter green thread and the upper side with both green threads. Blend from the darkest shade near the centre to the lightest on the outer edge. Stitch the centre vein with split stitch.

Top right hand leaf

Embroider this leaf in the same manner as the lower right hand leaf, omitting the straight stitch highlights.

Attaching the detached leaf

Cut out the leaf as close to the stitching as possible. Using the long darner, sink the wire at the marked position.

Bend the wire on the back of the work so it lies behind the leaf. Secure with overcast stitch and trim the excess wire.

Assembling the rose

Petals

Using the long darner, sink the wires for two of the largest petals first. Sink the medium petals next, so they are positioned in front of the large petals. Finally sink the small, then the tiny petals into the centre.

Secure the wires on the back of the work using overcast stitch. Trim the excess wire.

Shape the petals on the front so they curl under slightly, giving the impression of a rose in full bloom.

Centre

Stitch 8 - 10 ghiordes knots in the centre of the petals to form the stamens. Take care not to catch the petals and make the loops approximately 2.5cm (1") long. Trim the knots so they reach about halfway along the centre petals.

Cut a 40cm (15") length of the lighter red thread. Leaving a tail of thread approximately 10cm (4") long, wrap the bead until it is completely covered. Take the remaining tail of thread back through the stitches inside the bead and then take the two tails through the centre of the rose and stamens, to the back of the fabric. Secure on the back with tiny back stitches, ensuring it is very firm.

Spread the ghiordes knots evenly around the wrapped bead and rearrange the petals into the desired position.

EMBROIDERY KEY

All embroidery is worked with one strand of thread unless otherwise specified.

Stems and leaves

Main stem and large leaf stem = E (padded satin stitch)

Stem to left hand leaf = E (stem stitch)

New growth = E (satin stitch)

Leaf outlines on main fabric = D (split back stitch)

Leaves on main fabric = D and E (long and short stitch)

Leaf veins on main fabric = E (split stitch)

Highlights on lower right hand leaf = D (straight stitch)

Detached leaf = E (couching, overcasting, blanket stitch, long and short stitch)

Rose

Tiny, small and medium petals = B (couching, blanket stitch, long and short stitch), A (long and short stitch)

Large petals = A (couching, blanket stitch, long and short stitch), B (straight stitch)

Stamens = B blended with C (1 strand of each, Ghiordes knot)

Bead in centre of rose = B (wrapping)

Bud

Petals = A (padded satin stitch)

Calyx = E (split back stitch, long and short stitch, straight stitch)

Receptacle = E (split back stitch, padded satin stitch)

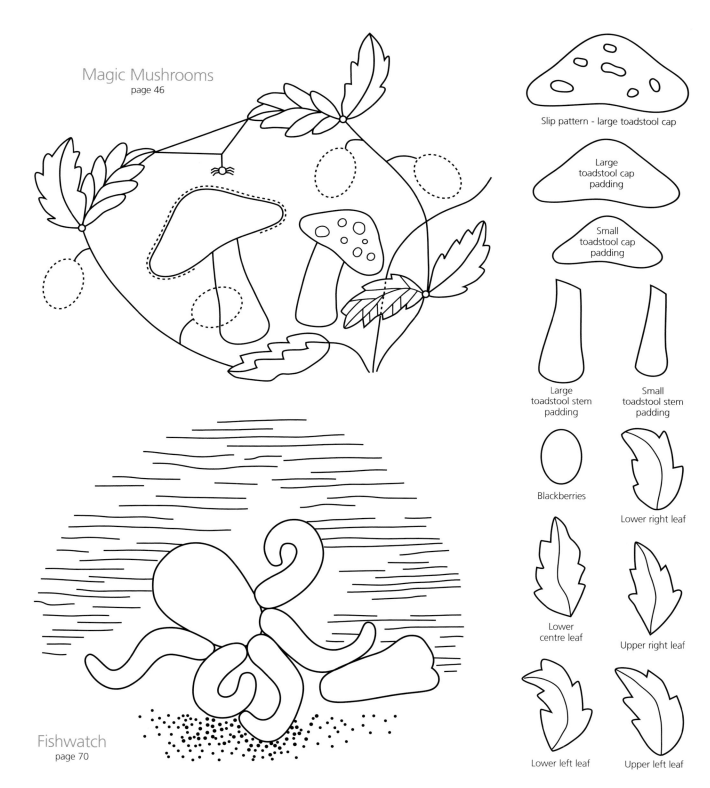

Magic Mushrooms
page 46

Slip pattern - large toadstool cap

Large toadstool cap padding

Small toadstool cap padding

Large toadstool stem padding

Small toadstool stem padding

Blackberries

Lower right leaf

Lower centre leaf

Upper right leaf

Lower left leaf

Upper left leaf

Fishwatch
page 70

113

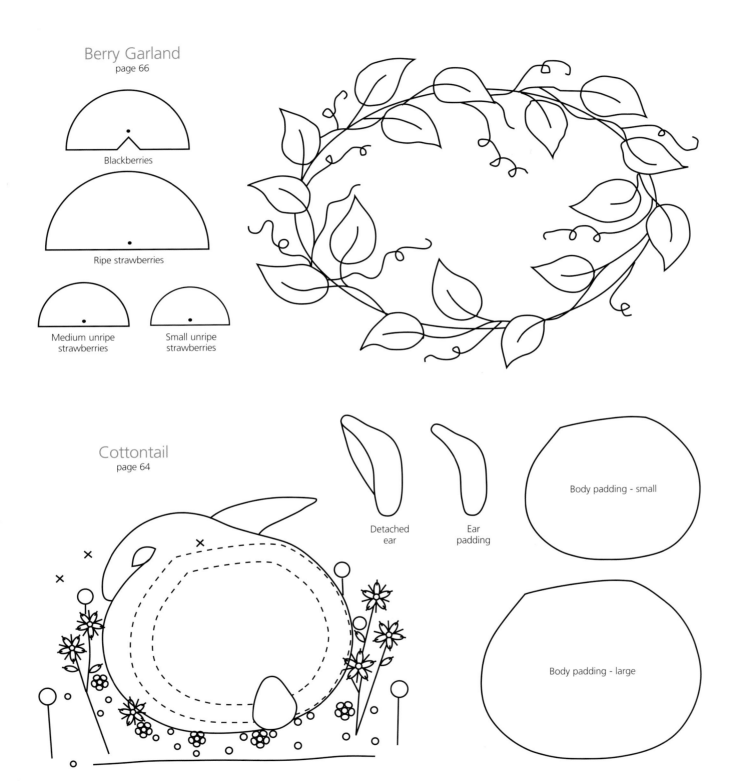

Berry Garland
page 66

Blackberries

Ripe strawberries

Medium unripe strawberries

Small unripe strawberries

Cottontail
page 64

Detached ear

Ear padding

Body padding - small

Body padding - large

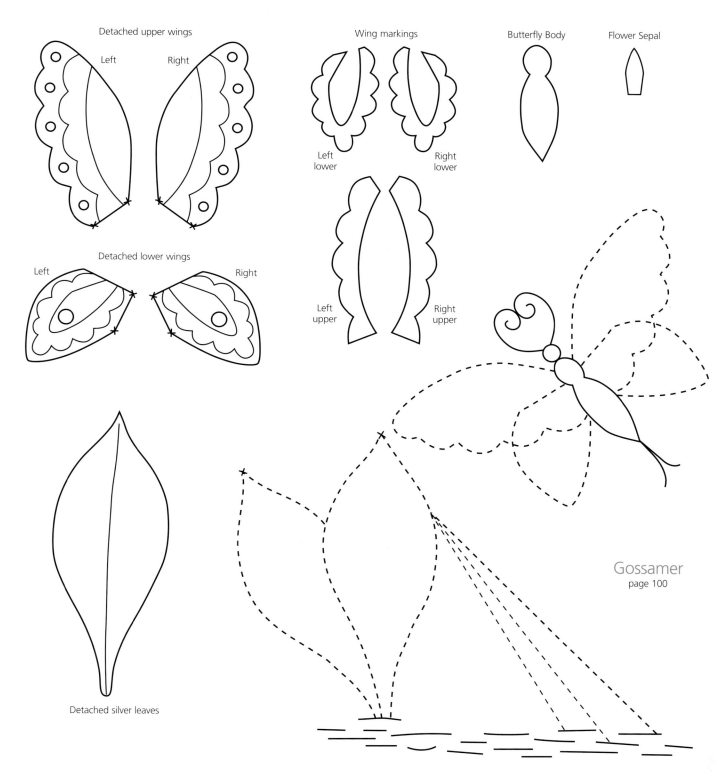

Detached upper wings

Left Right

Wing markings

Left lower Right lower

Butterfly Body

Flower Sepal

Detached lower wings

Left Right

Left upper Right upper

Detached silver leaves

Gossamer
page 100

115

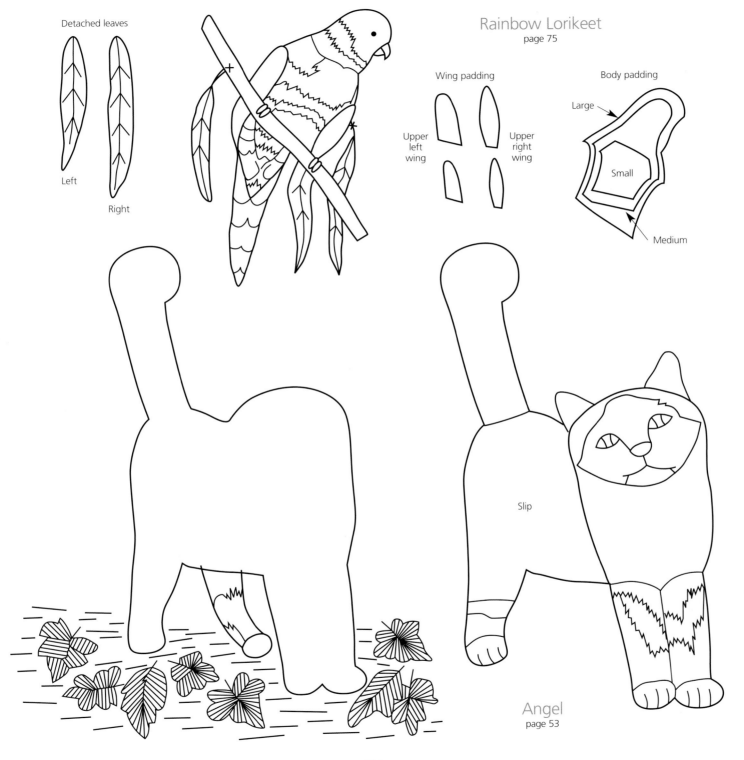

Detached leaves

Left

Right

Rainbow Lorikeet
page 75

Wing padding

Upper left wing

Upper right wing

Body padding

Large

Small

Medium

Slip

Angel
page 53

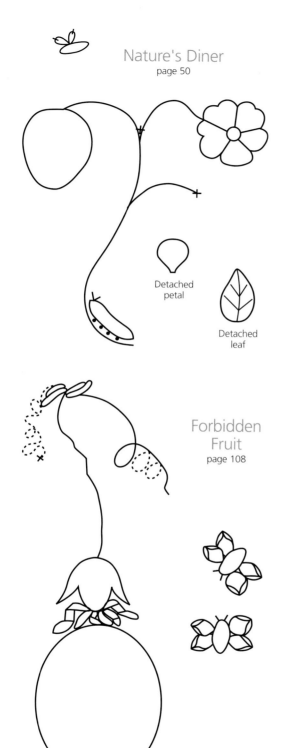

Nature's Diner
page 50

Detached
petal

Detached
leaf

Forbidden
Fruit
page 108

Christmas Bells
page 94

A

B

C

B

A

C

117

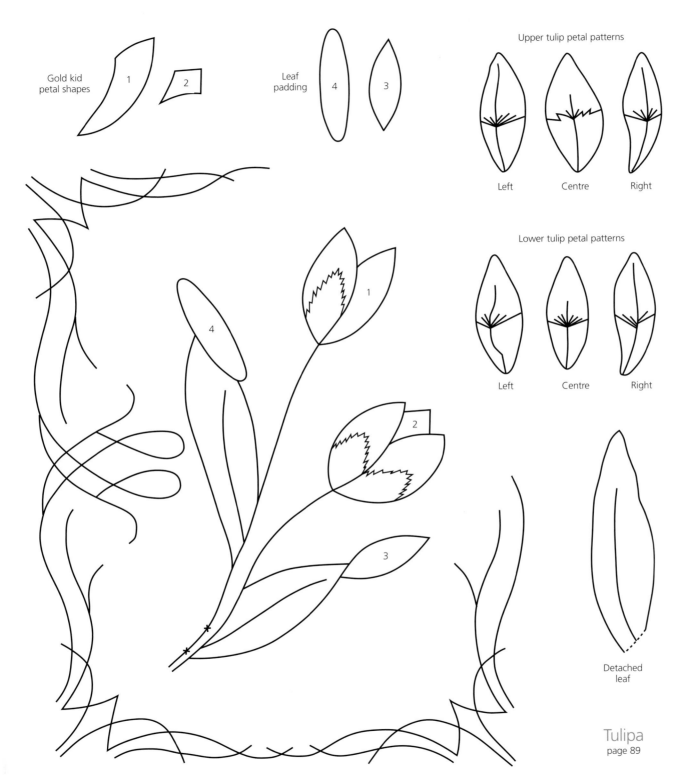

Gold kid
petal shapes

1

2

Leaf
padding

4

3

Upper tulip petal patterns

Left

Centre

Right

Lower tulip petal patterns

Left

Centre

Right

1

2

3

4

Detached
leaf

Tulipa
page 89

118

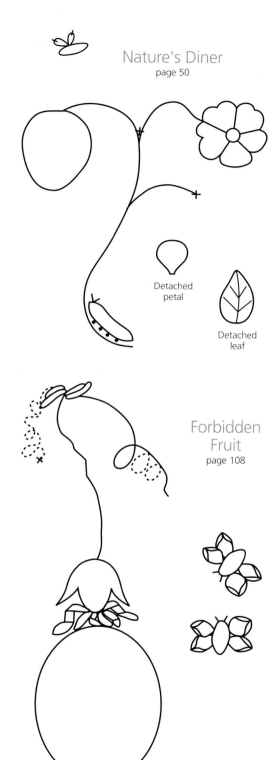

Nature's Diner
page 50

Detached petal

Detached leaf

Forbidden Fruit
page 108

Christmas Bells
page 94

A   B

C

B

A

C

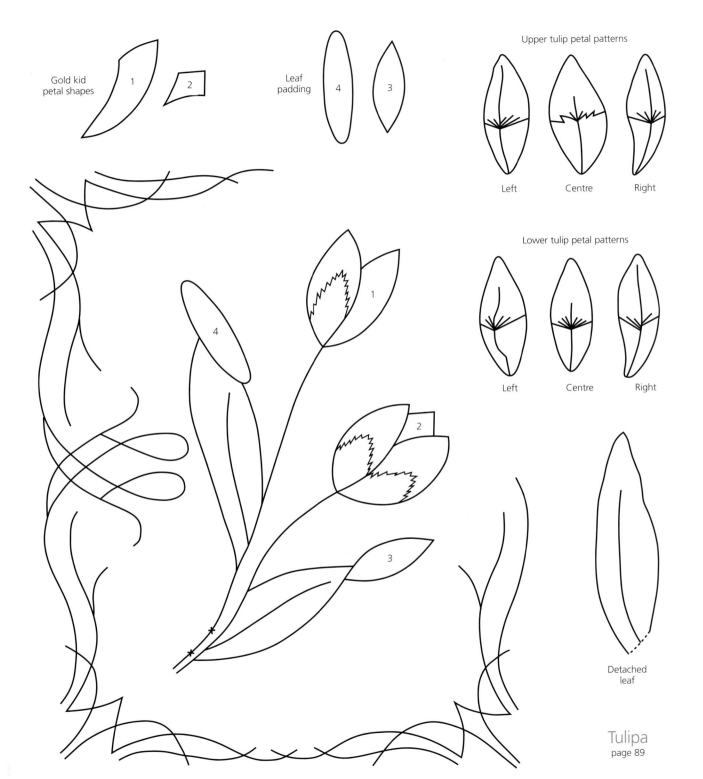

Gold kid
petal shapes

1

2

Leaf
padding

4

3

Upper tulip petal patterns

Left　　Centre　　Right

Lower tulip petal patterns

Left　　Centre　　Right

4

1

2

3

Detached
leaf

Tulipa
page 89

118

Wild Rose Garland
page 56

Rose petal pattern

Bee wing pattern

Bee shape diagram

Head padding large

Head padding small

Ball padding large

Ball padding small

Henry
page 72

Arm padding

Tummy padding small

Tummy padding large

Detached ears

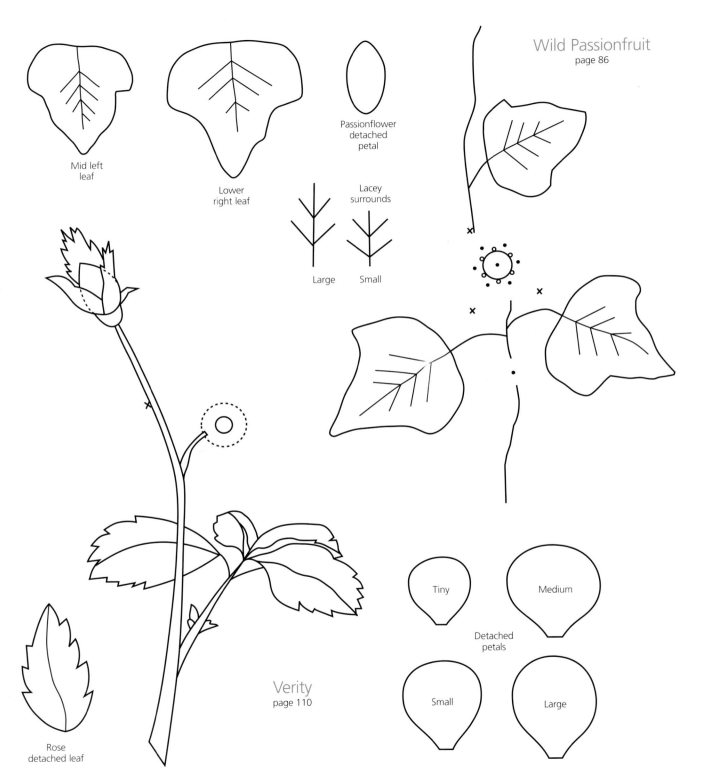

Mid left
leaf

Lower
right leaf

Passionflower
detached
petal

Lacey
surrounds

Large   Small

Wild Passionfruit
page 86

Verity
page 110

Rose
detached leaf

Tiny   Medium

Detached
petals

Small   Large

120

Geraldton Wax
page 92

Detached
side petals

Detached centre
petals

Gold kid
petal

Felt petal

Spring Splendour
page 97

B

A

Detached
petals

Detached
leaf

A

Left leaf tip
padding

B

Right leaf
tip padding

Left

Right

Moth lower wing patterns

Moth

Bee

Bee-eater
wing
padding

Bee-eater
body
padding

Dung
ball slip

Water
berry slip

Cream of
tartar fruit
slip

Baobab
tree leaf

Rhodesian
Holly leaf

Bee eater
leaf

Water
berry leaf

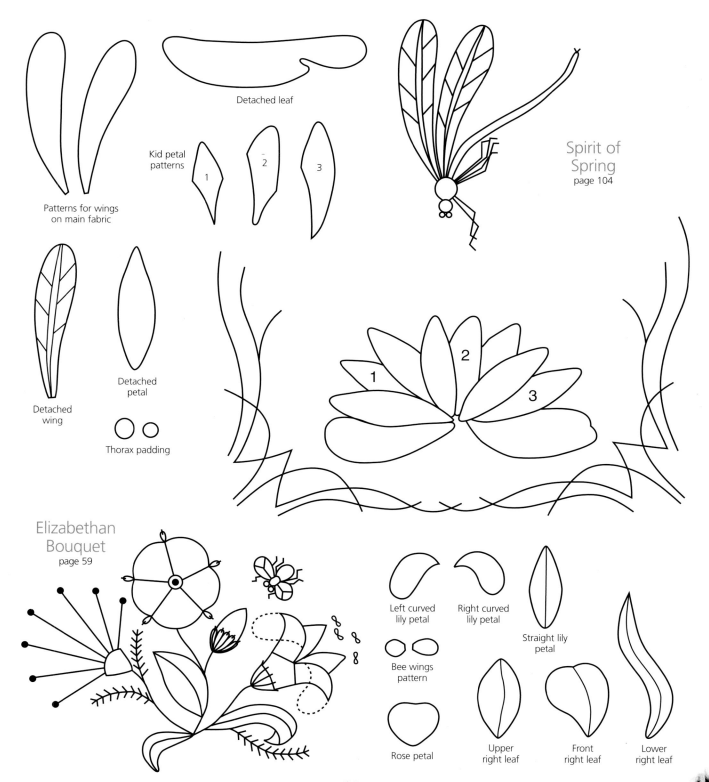

Detached leaf

Kid petal patterns

1

2

3

Patterns for wings on main fabric

Spirit of Spring
page 104

Detached wing

Detached petal

Thorax padding

1

2

3

Elizabethan Bouquet
page 59

Left curved lily petal

Right curved lily petal

Straight lily petal

Bee wings pattern

Rose petal

Upper right leaf

Front right leaf

Lower right leaf

NOTE:
Bold type denotes step-by-step instructions
Italics type denotes designers
Coloured type denotes designs

THE FABULOUS RANGE OF BOOKS AND MAGAZINES
FROM COUNTRY BUMPKIN

Needlework Books

Filled with beautiful projects,
easy instructions,
superb photography and
full size patterns.

Inspirations Baby

Inspirations Bridal

Inspirations Gifts

The World's Most Beautiful Blankets

Embroidered Christening Gowns

Embroidered Bags & Purses

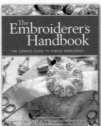
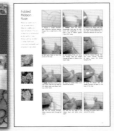

The Embroiderer's Handbook

The Embroidered Village Bag

Quarterly Magazines

Each magazine features
stunning projects, magnificent
photography, clear step-by-step
instructions and full size
patterns.

Inspirations

Australian Smocking & Embroidery

OTHER TITLES IN THE A-Z SERIES

Over 2,000,000 sold worldwide. The ultimate reference books for needleworkers.

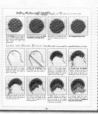

A-Z of Embroidery Stitches

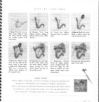

A-Z of Embroidered Flowers

A-Z of Bullions

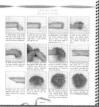

A-Z of Ribbon Embroidery

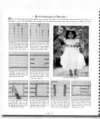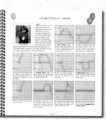

A-Z of Smocking

A-Z of Sewing for Smockers

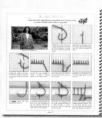

A-Z of Wool Embroidery

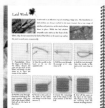

A-Z of Crewel Embroidery

If you would like more information on any Country Bumpkin title, please contact Country Bumpkin Publications:
315 Unley Road, Malvern, South Australia 5061
Phone: (08) 8372 7600 Fax: (08) 8372 7601 Email: mailorder@countrybumpkin.com.au
www.countrybumpkin.com.au

This book would not be possible without the
dedication and skill of the exceptionally talented
embroiderers whose work is featured here and
so we would like to say a very special thank you
to Trish Burr, Alison Cole, Helen Hardman,
Wendy Innes, Jan Kerton, Lizzie Kulinski, Janet Luce,
Annette Rich, Anna Scott, Judy Stephenson,
Lesley Turpin-Delport and Libby Vater.